Once More

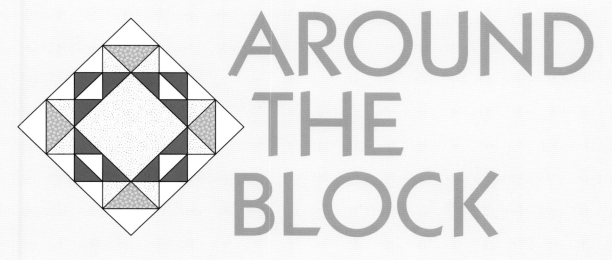

AROUND THE BLOCK

Judy Hopkins

Martingale®
& C O M P A N Y

Credits

President   Nancy J. Martin
CEO   Daniel J. Martin
Publisher   Jane Hamada
Editorial Director   Mary V. Green
Managing Editor   Tina Cook
Technical Editor   Laurie Baker
Copy Editor   Ellen Balstad
Design Director   Stan Green
Illustrator   Laurel Strand
Text Designer   Regina Girard
Cover Designer   Stan Green

That Patchwork Place® is an imprint
of Martingale & Company®.

Once More around the Block
© 2003 by Judy Hopkins

Martingale & Company
20205 144th Avenue NE
Woodinville, WA 98072-8478 USA
www.martingale-pub.com

Printed in China
08 07 06 05 04 03   8 7 6 5 4 3 2 1

Mission Statement

*Dedicated to providing quality products
and service to inspire creativity*

Library of Congress Cataloging-in-Publication Data

Hopkins, Judy.
    Once more around the block / Judy Hopkins.
      p. cm.
    ISBN 1-56477-492-9
  1. Patchwork—Patterns. 2. Quilting—Patterns.
I. Title.
    TT835 .H5698 2003
    746 .46'041—dc22

                              2003016637

Contents

Introduction

Some of my earliest quilting books were block reference books, and they are still among my favorites. I've spent many hours contentedly studying pieced blocks, learning their names, sketching them on graph paper, and figuring out how to cut and stitch them. My introduction to the wealth of traditional blocks was Mary Ellen Hopkins's *The It's Okay If You Sit on My Quilt Book.* Its delicious array of blocks was printed on graph paper, so you could see the underlying structure of the blocks. Later I expanded my block pattern horizons with Jinny Beyer's *The Quilter's Album of Blocks and Borders,* which came with a transparent overlay on which grids were printed. When I found Barbara Brackman's *Encyclopedia of Pieced Quilt Patterns*—first issued as a collection of loose-leaf pages—I was in block heaven! But in all of these wonderful resource books, something was missing: instructions for cutting and sewing the blocks.

Many block books, old and new, are reference books, geared toward pattern identification—tantalizing collections of possibilities that are out of reach of the quilter who is unwilling, or unable, to do the calculations necessary to translate line drawings into useable quick-cut blocks. Block-pattern books are available, but in many of these the pattern for each block is given in just one size. The same is true of most block patterns published in quilting magazines.

This block book—the third in the Around the Block series—is different. Designed for the quilter who loves both old patterns and modern rotary-cutting techniques, it provides clear, complete instructions in multiple sizes for each of 200 classic blocks. These blocks do not appear in the two earlier Around the Block books.

Brief how-to sections take you from quilt planning through borders, but the emphasis here is on blocks: a smorgasbord of popular patterns that you can quickly cut and piece in the size of your choice.

Using the Block Patterns

The block patterns appear in alphabetical order. Many blocks have more than one familiar name; a block you commonly refer to as Barbara Frietchie Star may be known by other quilters as Pierced Star or Star Puzzle. If you don't readily find the block you are looking for, it may appear under a different name. Sometimes one block may be identical to another block in the size, shape, and placement of its pieces, but because the arrangement of values (lights, mediums, and darks) is different, it will have a different name. Compare Fireflies and Goose and Goslings, for instance. The pieces are exactly the same, but the value arrangements are different, and each version has a unique name.

Block designs typically are drafted on regular underlying grids. For example, a six-unit block is based on a grid that is six squares across and six down. In this book, a grid notation is included as part of each pattern.

Each block pattern includes a shaded drawing and a lettered drawing, both keyed to the cutting instructions, and a piecing diagram.

Most of the patterns produce a single block. For a few of the blocks, it is a more efficient use of fabric to cut the pieces for two or even four blocks at a time. *Check each pattern to see how many blocks the instructions will yield.*

You can choose from one of six different finished sizes for each block. The finished sizes range from 4" to 15⅛", depending on the particular block and the number of units it contains. You will find cutting instructions for the "standard" 12" block in some, but not all, of the patterns. Blocks based on 5-, 7-, 9-, 10- and 11-unit grids simply do not translate well to a 12" format, as 12 is not divisible into quarters or eighths by 5, 7, 9, 10, or 11. It would be difficult to accurately measure and cut the 3.1666" and 3.9166" squares that might be needed to make a 12" block from a design based on a 9-unit grid!

Hour Glass IV

6-Unit Grid

Color Illustration: page 21

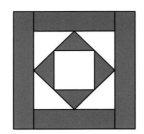 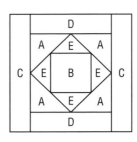 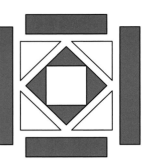

For 1 block:			FINISHED BLOCK SIZE					
			Single dimensions in the cutting chart indicate the size of the cut square (3" = 3" x 3").					
			4½"	6"	7½"	9"	10½"	12"
Light	A: 2 ◻▸◣		2⅜"	2⅞"	3⅜"	3⅞"	4⅜"	4⅞"
	B: 1 ◻		2"	2½"	3"	3½"	4"	4½"
Dark	C: 2 ▭		1¼" x 5"	1½" x 6½"	1¾" x 8"	2" x 9½"	2¼" x 11"	2½" x 12½"
	D: 2 ▭		1¼" x 3½"	1½" x 4½"	1¾" x 5½"	2" x 6½"	2¼" x 7½"	2½" x 8½"
	E: 1 ⊠▸⧖		2¾"	3¼"	3¾"	4¼"	4¾"	5¼"

Try this: Reverse the lights and darks in every other block.

Cutting the Blocks

The block cutting directions are displayed in charts. These instructions are easy to follow once you are familiar with the terms and notations used throughout the book. Let's use the Hour Glass IV pattern as an example. Note that the block is based on a six–unit grid, and that the cutting instructions produce one block.

The general instructions for this block call for a light fabric and a dark fabric. Refer to the shaded drawing to see where these values appear in the block. Some of the block patterns call for three values: light, medium, and dark. Others may require two different light fabrics (light and light 2) and/or two different medium fabrics (medium and medium 2) to define the pattern. When a pattern calls for two lights or two mediums, you could use two different prints of the same color or two different colors of the same value.

Letters identify the various pattern pieces to cut. Check the lettered drawing to see where each of these pieces appears in the block.

In the cutting chart, a number and an icon follow each piece's letter designation. The number tells you *how many pieces* to cut, and the icon tells you *what to cut*. Four simple icons are used throughout the book:

◻ = Square(s)

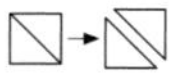

◻▸◣ = Square(s) cut once diagonally to make half-square triangles

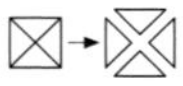

⊠▸⧖ = Square(s) cut twice diagonally to make quarter-square triangles

▭ = Rectangle(s)

If the general cutting instruction says "A: 2 ◻," cut two squares. If the cutting instruction says "B: 2 ◻▸◣," cut two squares, and then cut the squares once diagonally to make the four piece B half-square triangles needed for the block. If the cutting instruction says "C: 1 ⊠▸⊠," cut one square, and then cut the square twice diagonally to make the four piece C quarter-square triangles required. If the cutting instruction says "D: 2 ▭," cut two rectangles.

The cutting dimensions for the pieces appear in the columns to the right of the general cutting instructions and include ¼"-wide seam allowances; *do not add seam allowances to the measurements given.* For example, if you want to make an Hour Glass IV block that finishes to 9", follow the general cutting instructions, using the dimensions given in the 9" finished-block-size column:

◆ The first cutting instruction (A: 2 ◸▸◺) tells you to cut two squares from the light fabric and to cut each square once diagonally to make a total of four half-square triangles. For a 9" block, cut 3⅞" x 3⅞" squares.

◆ The second cutting instruction (B: 1 ☐) tells you to cut one square from the light fabric. For a 9" block, cut a 3½" x 3½" square.

◆ The third cutting instruction (C: 2 ▭) tells you to cut two rectangles from the dark fabric. For a 9" block, cut two 2" x 9½" rectangles.

◆ The fourth cutting instruction (D: 2 ▭) tells you to cut two more rectangles from the dark fabric; these rectangles are shorter than the C rectangles above. For a 9" block, cut two 2" x 6½" rectangles.

◆ The final cutting instruction (E: 1 ⊠▸⊠) tells you to cut one square from the dark fabric and to cut the square twice diagonally to make a total of four quarter-square triangles. For a 9" block, cut 4¼" x 4¼" squares.

Variations

Each block pattern includes a "Try this" notation that suggests a variation on the block. For the Hour Glass IV block, I suggest reversing the lights and darks in every other block. This means that for your second block, you would cut A and B from the dark fabric and C, D, and E from the light.

Sometimes a "Try this" note will say something like "Use several different mediums for E." Increasing the number of fabrics used in the block while retaining the suggested value arrangement is a strategy worth considering for any of the block patterns. For example, you could cut A from one light fabric and B from a different light for the Hour Glass IV block. These could be two prints of the same color (or similar in color) but different in design scale or visual texture. Or, you could use two different colors, both light.

Note that the "Try this" note for one block might well apply to several others. Read through the "Try this" notations throughout the book to get more ideas. Many other variations are possible. For example, consider combining lights and mediums or mediums and darks instead of lights and darks to vary the contrast. Play with value placement to create blocks with an entirely different look.

Rotary Cutting Individual Pieces

When cutting just a few pieces from a single fabric, use a small cutting ruler like the Bias Square®. If you want to cut several pieces at one time, fold or stack the fabric into as many as four layers. Place the Bias Square on one corner of the fabric, aligning the edges with the fabric grain (sometimes it is easier to see the grain from the wrong side of the fabric). If the fabric edges are uneven, make sure that the ruler markings for the dimensions you wish to cut do not extend beyond the fabric or overlap the selvage. For example, if you need a 2¾" square, make sure the 2¾" markings on the Bias Square are well within the fabric edges. Cut the first two sides. Rotate your cutting mat or turn the cut piece of fabric. Align the proper measurement on the Bias Square along the edges you just cut, and cut the opposite two sides.

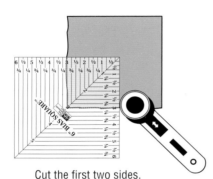

Cut the first two sides.

Cut the opposite two sides.

Tip Often, when I need just one or two pieces from a particular fabric, I leave the fabric folded just as it comes from my shelf. I slide a small cutting mat between the layers and cut out the corner or a short strip without disturbing my careful folds.

Stitching Tips for Square-in-a-Square Units

1. Join the opposing triangles first, centering the triangles on the square. The triangle points will be sticking out about ⅜" beyond the edges of the square. Press seams toward the triangles.

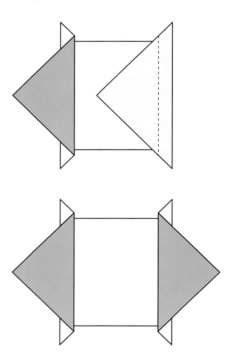

2. Join the remaining triangles to the square. Your ¼" seam should exactly intersect the 90° angle where the two triangles meet at both the top and bottom ends of the seam, as in the magnified areas of the drawing.

Adjust the position of the loose triangle until the seam lines up correctly at A. Take a few stitches. Then adjust the points at B and finish stitching the seam. Press seams toward the triangles.

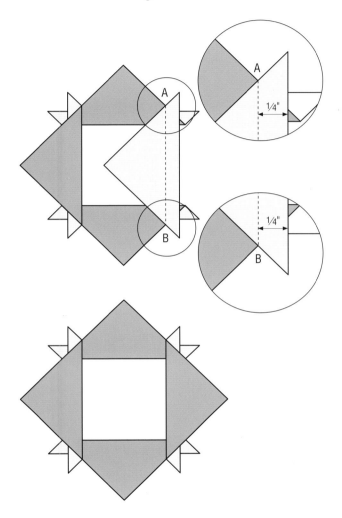

Stitching Tips for Flying-Geese Units

1. Join the left-hand triangle: Match points (A) and bottom edges; sew in the direction of the arrow. Press seam toward the smaller triangle.

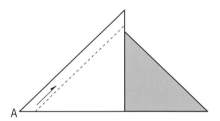

2. Join the right-hand triangle. Start at the arrow. Your ¼" seam should exactly intersect the 90° angle where the two smaller triangles meet, as in the magnified portion of the drawing. Adjust the position of the loose triangle until the seam lines up correctly. Take a few stitches, then match points (B) and finish stitching the seam. Press seam toward the smaller triangle.

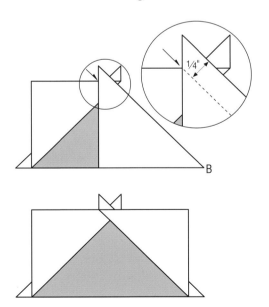

Planning Your Quilt

You almost certainly will want to use these patterns to make quilts, not just blocks. Some quilters plan their quilts before they begin making blocks; others construct a number of blocks before they decide how to set them together into a quilt. Whichever approach you take, there are numerous setting options to consider. Work with your blocks or with photocopies of a shaded block drawing. Try several different arrangements: side by side, side by side with every other block rotated, on point, with plain or pieced alternate blocks, or with plain or pieced sashing. Or consider a strippy arrangement, with horizontal or vertical bands of blocks separated by plain or pieced bars. You'll find lots of ideas in *Sensational Settings: Over 80 Ways to Arrange Your Quilt Blocks* by Joan Hanson (Martingale & Company, 2004).

While some quilts are planned so that the pattern or design extends to the outside edges, most quilts have a patterned center section surrounded by borders. Decisions you make about the size, number, and layout of the blocks will determine the size of the patterned section of your quilt. The border width will establish the final dimensions. If you are making a quilt for the wall, the design and proportion of the piece are often more important than the size. Quilts for beds, on the other hand, must be made to a specific size.

Once I've chosen a setting arrangement, I sketch out a quilt plan on a work sheet like one of those provided on pages 139–140. This makes it easy for me to calculate the size of the patterned section of the quilt and to count the number of blocks and setting pieces I will need. For bed quilts, I plan the patterned section of the quilt, and then I select a border width that will bring the quilt to the desired finished dimensions. I work within general size guidelines that give me some room for design flexibility.

Quilt Size Guidelines

	Width	Length
Baby	36"–45"	45"–54"
Crib	42"–48"	54"–60"
Nap	54"–60"	68"–76"
Twin	56"–64"	84"–100"
Double	70"–80"	84"–100"
Queen	76"–84"	90"–104"
King	92"–100"	90"–104"

Making Multiple Blocks

When you use these block patterns to make a repeat-block quilt, you will not want to cut out the blocks one at a time. Instead, multiply the numbers in the cutting-instruction column by the number of blocks you wish to make, and cut all the identical pieces at the same time. Before you do these calculations, check to see if the block pattern yields more than one block. The Hour Glass IV pattern on page 81 produces one block. To make 20 Hour Glass IV blocks, multiply the numbers in the cutting-instruction column by 20, and cut 40 A, 20 B, 40 C, 40 D and 20 E. To make 20 blocks from a pattern that yields 2 blocks, multiply the numbers in the cutting-instruction column by 10, not 20.

When cutting many identical pieces from a single fabric, common practice is to cut selvage-to-selvage strips to the proper width, and then subcut the strips into squares or rectangles. For a refresher on basic rotary-cutting techniques, refer to *Shortcuts: A Concise Guide to Rotary Cutting* by Donna Lynn Thomas (Martingale & Company, 1999).

Remember, it is always wise to make a sample block to test the pattern and confirm your fabric choices before cutting up yards of fabric!

When you make several blocks from a single pattern, watch for opportunities to use quick triangle-piecing techniques, strip-piecing methods, or other shortcuts from your own arsenal of tricks. A number of the blocks in this book contain four-patch units, for instance. Construct them with your favorite strip-piecing method instead of cutting and joining the individual squares.

Calculating Yardage Requirements

The first step in calculating yardage requirements for multiple blocks is to figure out how many of each shape you can get from a selvage-to-selvage strip cut to one of the shape's dimensions. Pattern writers commonly count on 42" of usable width from commercial fabrics. So if you need a total of forty 2" x 2" squares, first determine how many squares you can get from one 2" x 42" strip. Divide 42" by 2 to get 21.

Next, determine how many strips you will need. Divide the total number of squares needed (40) by the number of squares per strip (21) and round up to the next whole number to get 2.

Finally, multiply the cut width of the strips (2") by the number of strips needed (2) to get 4".

Do these calculations for each of the shapes, and then add the results to find the total number of inches needed from each fabric. I usually add 10% to the total, to allow for fabric shrinkage and distortion, and then divide the final figure by 36 to determine the total yardage required.

Let's calculate the total amount of light fabric needed for twenty 9" Hour Glass IV blocks as an example (refer to the cutting instructions on page 81).

Piece A:
For 20 blocks, you need 40 squares,
    each 3⅞" x 3⅞".
One strip, 3⅞" x 42", yields 10 squares
    (42 divided by 3.875 = 10.84).
You need 4 strips to get 40 squares
    (40 divided by 10 = 4).
So, you need 15½" of fabric for A
    (3.875" multiplied by 4).

Piece B:
For 20 blocks, you need 20 squares,
    each 3½" x 3½".
One strip, 3½" x 42", yields 12 squares
    (42 divided by 3.5 = 12).
You need 2 strips to get 20 squares
    (20 divided by 12 = 1.66, rounded
    up to the nearest whole number).
So, you need 7" of fabric for B
    (3.5" multiplied by 2).

The total yardage needed for pieces A and B is 22.5". Adding 10% (2.25") to allow for distortion and shrinkage brings the final figure to 24.75", or about ¾ yard of a light fabric.

Decimal-to-Inch Conversions

.0625 = ¹⁄₁₆"

.125 = ⅛"

.1875 = ³⁄₁₆"

.25 = ¼"

.3125 = ⁵⁄₁₆"

.375 = ⅜"

.4375 = ⁷⁄₁₆"

.5 = ½"

.5625 = ⁹⁄₁₆"

.625 = ⅝"

.6875 = ¹¹⁄₁₆"

.75 = ¾"

.8125 = ¹³⁄₁₆"

.875 = ⅞"

.9375 = ¹⁵⁄₁₆"

Gallery of Blocks

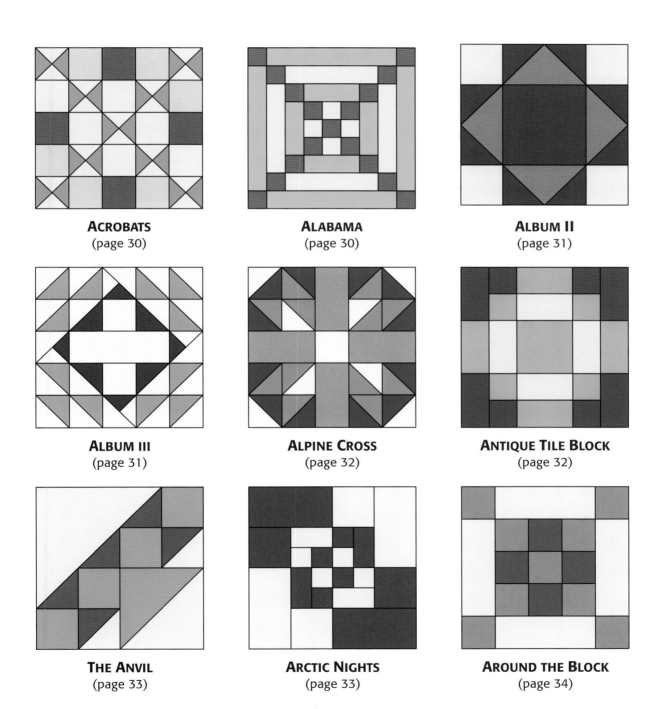

ACROBATS
(page 30)

ALABAMA
(page 30)

ALBUM II
(page 31)

ALBUM III
(page 31)

ALPINE CROSS
(page 32)

ANTIQUE TILE BLOCK
(page 32)

THE ANVIL
(page 33)

ARCTIC NIGHTS
(page 33)

AROUND THE BLOCK
(page 34)

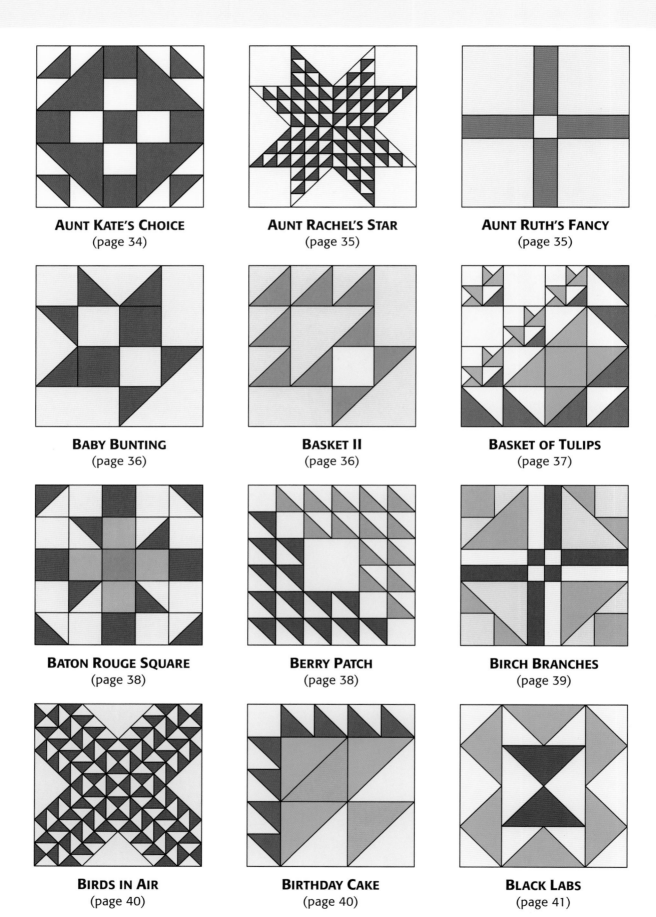

AUNT KATE'S CHOICE
(page 34)

AUNT RACHEL'S STAR
(page 35)

AUNT RUTH'S FANCY
(page 35)

BABY BUNTING
(page 36)

BASKET II
(page 36)

BASKET OF TULIPS
(page 37)

BATON ROUGE SQUARE
(page 38)

BERRY PATCH
(page 38)

BIRCH BRANCHES
(page 39)

BIRDS IN AIR
(page 40)

BIRTHDAY CAKE
(page 40)

BLACK LABS
(page 41)

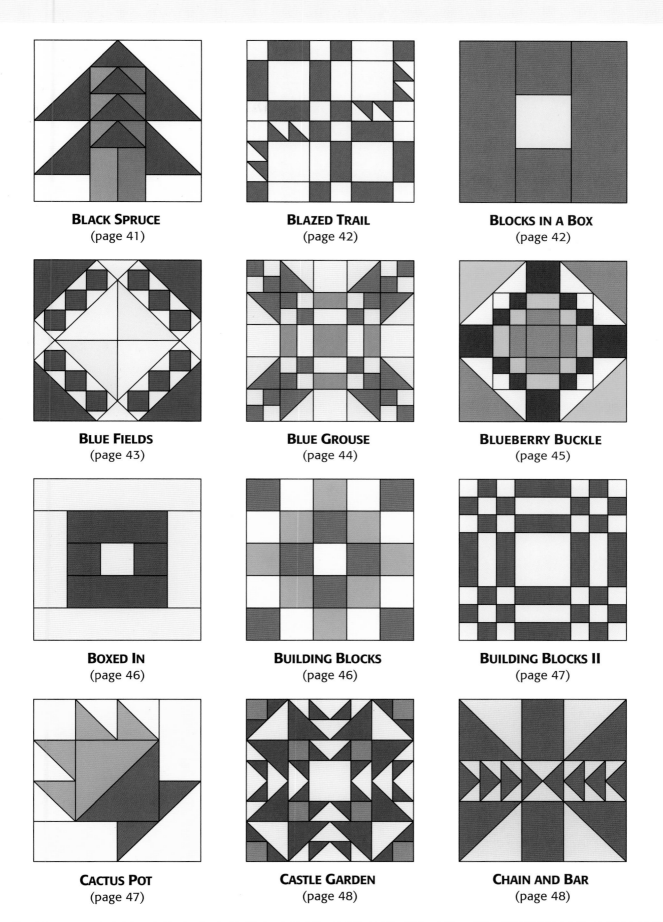

BLACK SPRUCE
(page 41)

BLAZED TRAIL
(page 42)

BLOCKS IN A BOX
(page 42)

BLUE FIELDS
(page 43)

BLUE GROUSE
(page 44)

BLUEBERRY BUCKLE
(page 45)

BOXED IN
(page 46)

BUILDING BLOCKS
(page 46)

BUILDING BLOCKS II
(page 47)

CACTUS POT
(page 47)

CASTLE GARDEN
(page 48)

CHAIN AND BAR
(page 48)

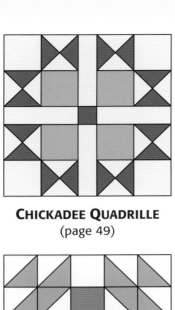

CHICKADEE QUADRILLE
(page 49)

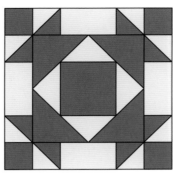

THE CHINESE BLOCK QUILT
(page 49)

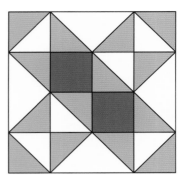

CHISHOLM TRAIL
(page 50)

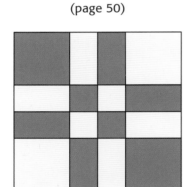

CHRISTMAS STAR II
(page 50)

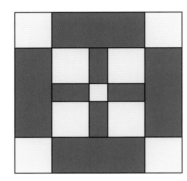

THE COMFORT QUILT
(page 51)

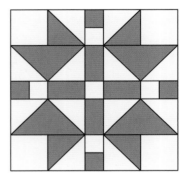

THE CONTINENTAL
(page 51)

COUNTERCHANGE CROSS
(page 52)

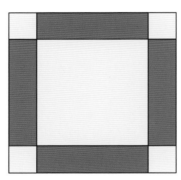

COUNTERPANE
(page 52)

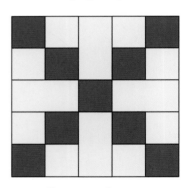

COUNTRY LANES
(page 53)

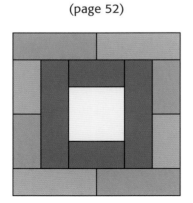

THE CRAYON BOX
(page 53)

CRAZY ANN
(page 54)

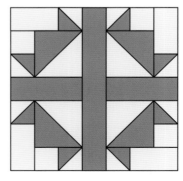

CROSS AND CROWN
(page 54)

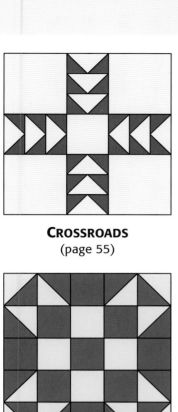

CROSSROADS
(page 55)

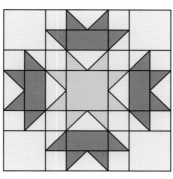

CROWN AND STAR
(page 55)

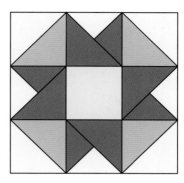

CRY OF THE LOON
(page 56)

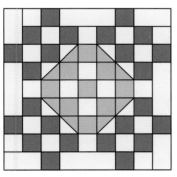

DEWEY DREAM QUILT
(page 56)

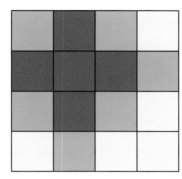

DIAGONAL SQUARE
(page 57)

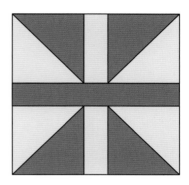

DIAMOND PANES
(page 57)

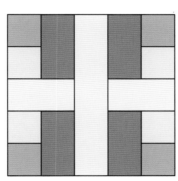

DIAMOND PLAID BLOCK
(page 58)

DOES DOUBLE DUTY
(page 58)

DOMINO NET
(page 59)

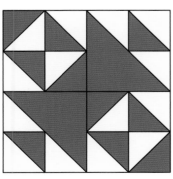

DOUBLE CROSS II
(page 59)

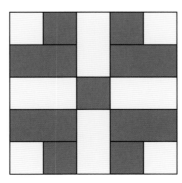

THE DOUBLE V
(page 60)

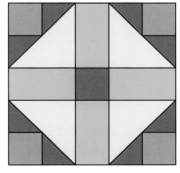

DUCK'S FOOT
(page 60)

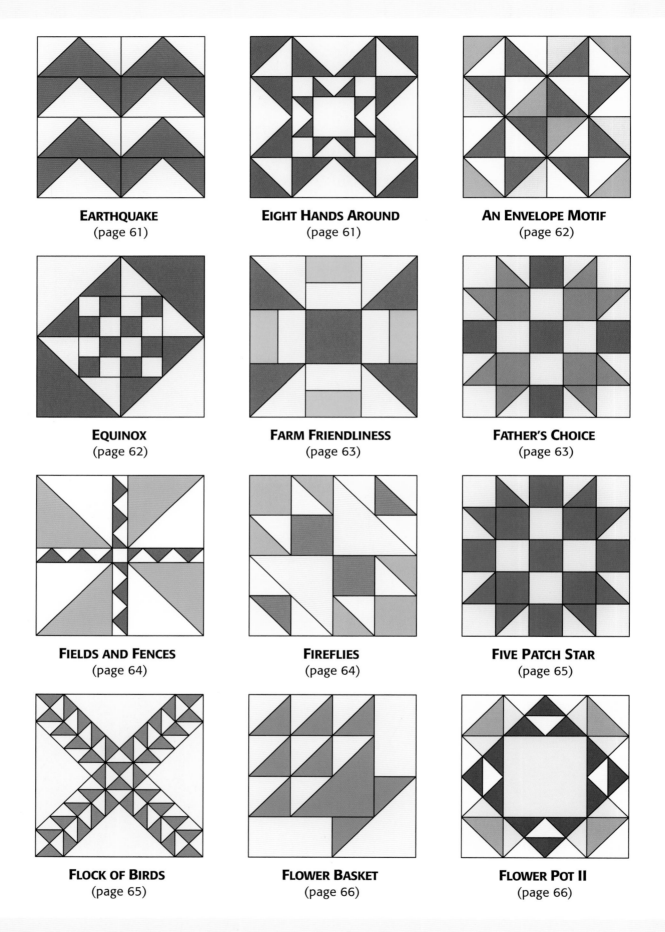

EARTHQUAKE
(page 61)

EIGHT HANDS AROUND
(page 61)

AN ENVELOPE MOTIF
(page 62)

EQUINOX
(page 62)

FARM FRIENDLINESS
(page 63)

FATHER'S CHOICE
(page 63)

FIELDS AND FENCES
(page 64)

FIREFLIES
(page 64)

FIVE PATCH STAR
(page 65)

FLOCK OF BIRDS
(page 65)

FLOWER BASKET
(page 66)

FLOWER POT II
(page 66)

FLYFOOT
(page 67)

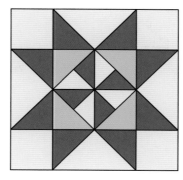

FLYING CLOUD
(page 67)

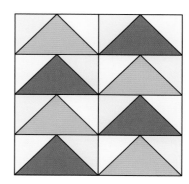

FLYING GEESE II
(page 68)

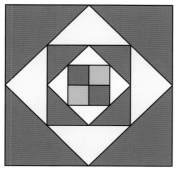

FOGGY MOUNTAIN BREAKDOWN
(page 68)

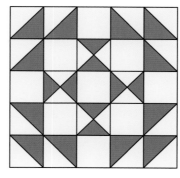

FOOT STOOL
(page 69)

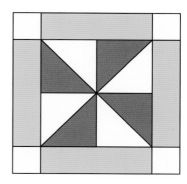

FOREST PATHS
(page 69)

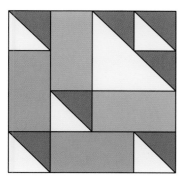

FORGET-ME-NOTS
(page 70)

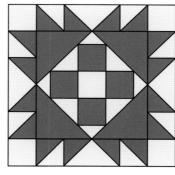

FOXY GRANDPA
(page 70)

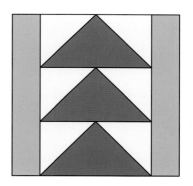

GAGGLE OF GEESE
(page 71)

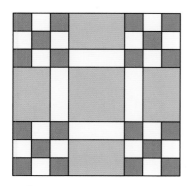

GLORIFIED NINE PATCH
(page 71)

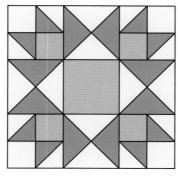

GOLDEN SAMOVAR
(page 72)

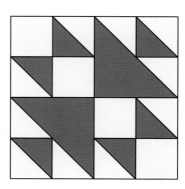

GOOSE AND GOSLINGS
(page 72)

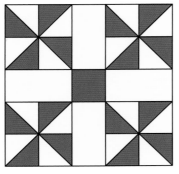

GRANDMA'S FAVORITE
(page 73)

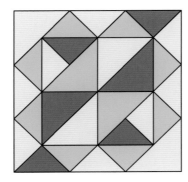

GRANDMA'S HOP SCOTCH QUILT
(page 73)

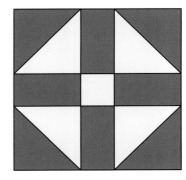

GRANDMOTHER'S CHOICE II
(page 74)

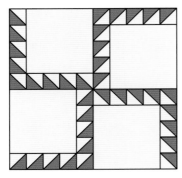

GRANDMOTHER'S PINWHEEL
(page 74)

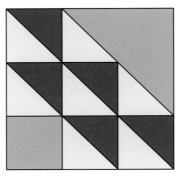

GREAT BLUE HERON
(page 75)

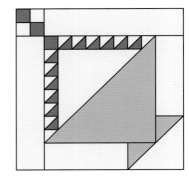

HANGING BASKET
(page 75)

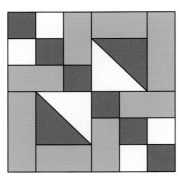

HAYES CORNER
(page 76)

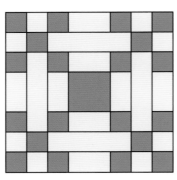

THE HEN AND HER CHICKS
(page 76)

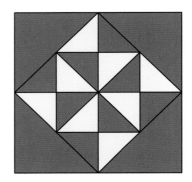

HERM'S SHIRT
(page 77)

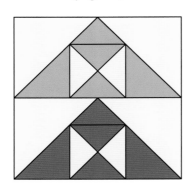

HILL AND VALLEY
(page 77)

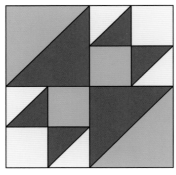

HOLLIS STAR
(page 78)

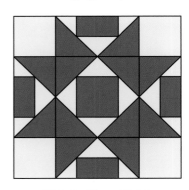

HOME TREASURE
(page 78)

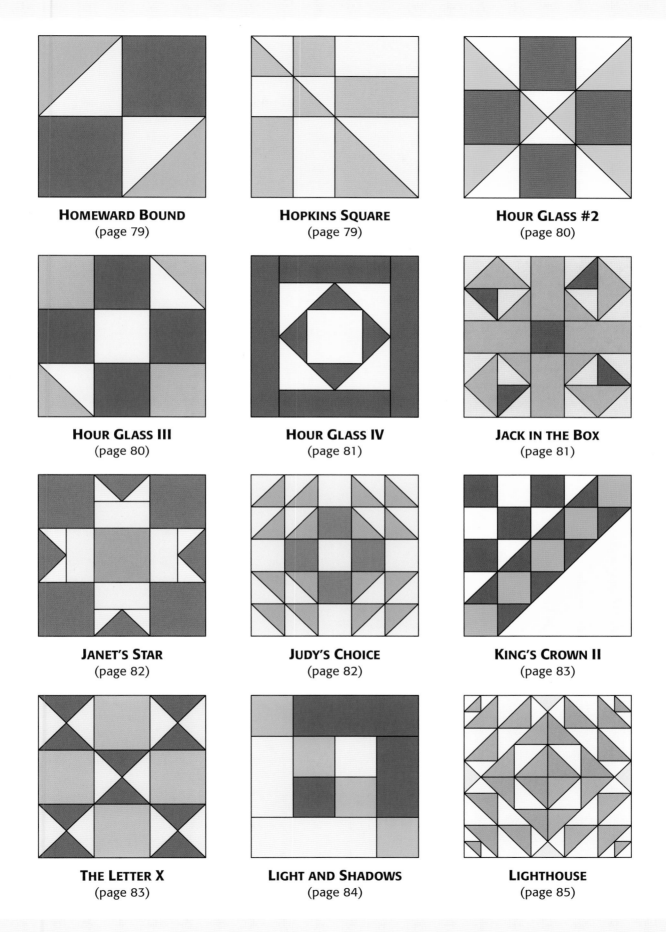

HOMEWARD BOUND
(page 79)

HOPKINS SQUARE
(page 79)

HOUR GLASS #2
(page 80)

HOUR GLASS III
(page 80)

HOUR GLASS IV
(page 81)

JACK IN THE BOX
(page 81)

JANET'S STAR
(page 82)

JUDY'S CHOICE
(page 82)

KING'S CROWN II
(page 83)

THE LETTER X
(page 83)

LIGHT AND SHADOWS
(page 84)

LIGHTHOUSE
(page 85)

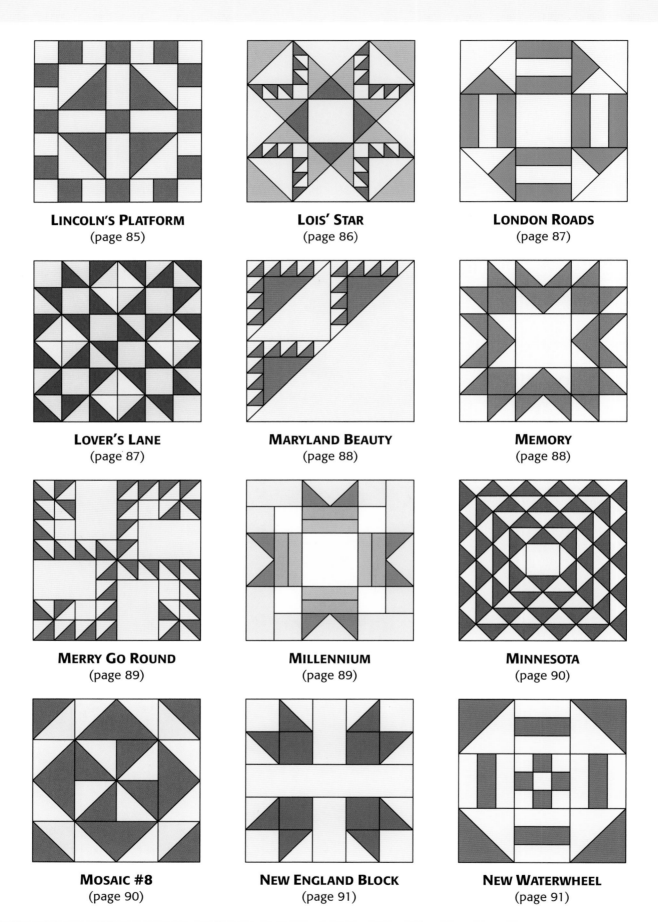

LINCOLN'S PLATFORM
(page 85)

LOIS' STAR
(page 86)

LONDON ROADS
(page 87)

LOVER'S LANE
(page 87)

MARYLAND BEAUTY
(page 88)

MEMORY
(page 88)

MERRY GO ROUND
(page 89)

MILLENNIUM
(page 89)

MINNESOTA
(page 90)

MOSAIC #8
(page 90)

NEW ENGLAND BLOCK
(page 91)

NEW WATERWHEEL
(page 91)

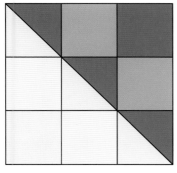

NINE PATCH STRAIGHT FURROW
(page 92)

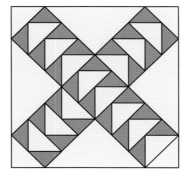

THE NORTH CAROLINA BEAUTY
(page 92)

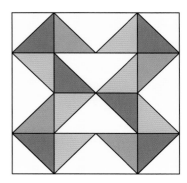

OLD GREY GOOSE
(page 93)

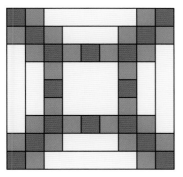

ON THE SQUARE
(page 93)

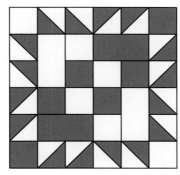

ONE MORE BLOCK
(page 94)

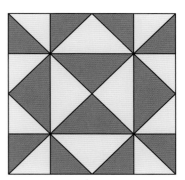

OUR EDITOR
(page 94)

THE OZARK TRAIL
(page 95)

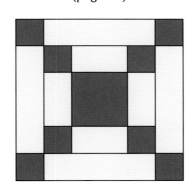

PENNSYLVANIA
(page 95)

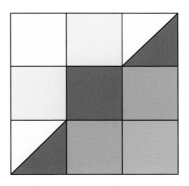

PERKIOMEN VALLEY
(page 96)

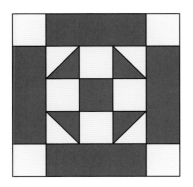

PHILADELPHIA PAVEMENT
(page 96)

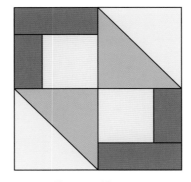

PICKET FENCE
(page 97)

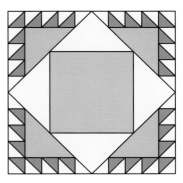

PINE BURR
(page 97)

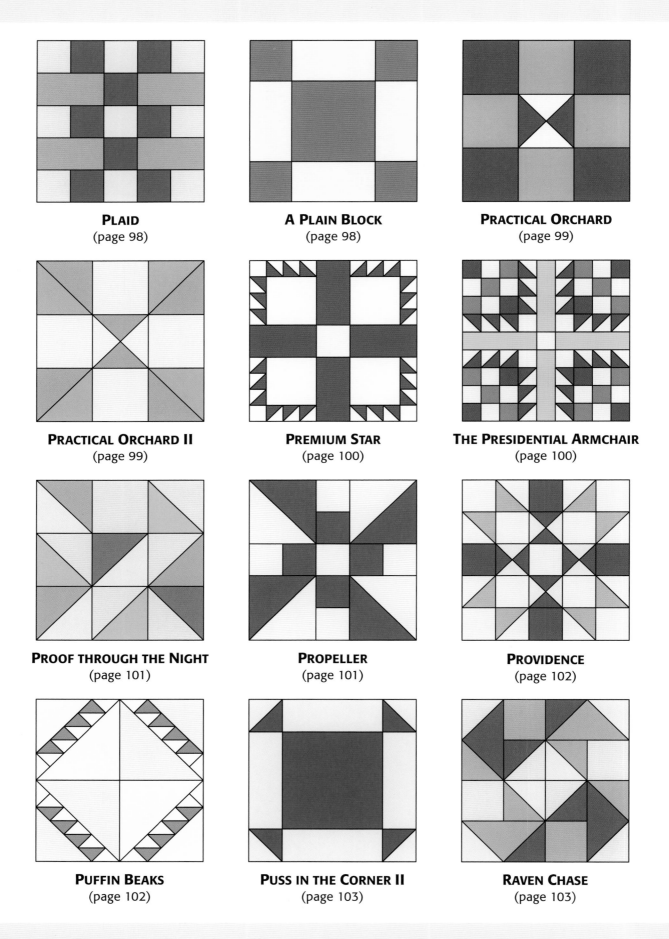

PLAID
(page 98)

A PLAIN BLOCK
(page 98)

PRACTICAL ORCHARD
(page 99)

PRACTICAL ORCHARD II
(page 99)

PREMIUM STAR
(page 100)

THE PRESIDENTIAL ARMCHAIR
(page 100)

PROOF THROUGH THE NIGHT
(page 101)

PROPELLER
(page 101)

PROVIDENCE
(page 102)

PUFFIN BEAKS
(page 102)

PUSS IN THE CORNER II
(page 103)

RAVEN CHASE
(page 103)

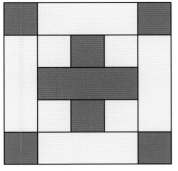

RED CROSS II
(page 104)

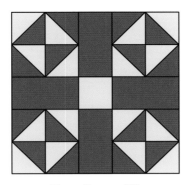

RED CROSS III
(page 104)

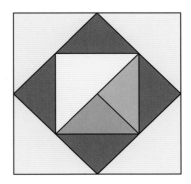

REMEMBER ME
(page 105)

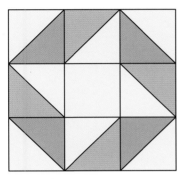

RIBBON QUILT
(page 105)

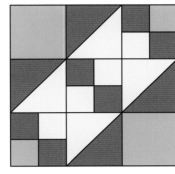

ROAD TO THE WHITE HOUSE
(page 106)

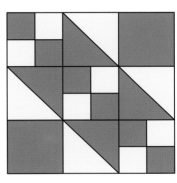

ROCKY ROAD TO CALIFORNIA
(page 106)

ROCKY ROAD TO DUBLIN
(page 107)

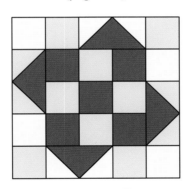

ROLLING NINE PATCH
(page 107)

ROLLING PINWHEEL
(page 108)

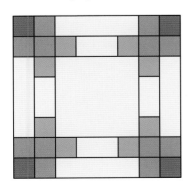

THE ROSEBUD
(page 108)

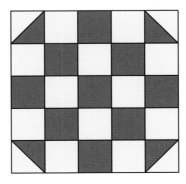

ROUND THE CORNER
(page 109)

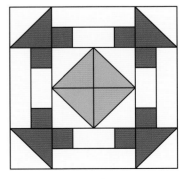

RUINS OF JERICHO
(page 109)

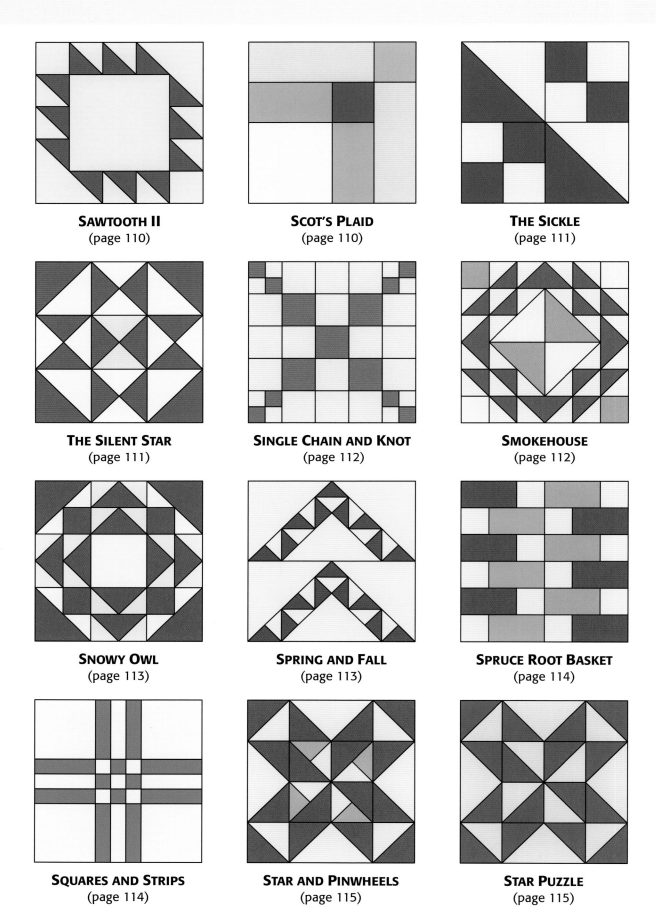

SAWTOOTH II
(page 110)

SCOT'S PLAID
(page 110)

THE SICKLE
(page 111)

THE SILENT STAR
(page 111)

SINGLE CHAIN AND KNOT
(page 112)

SMOKEHOUSE
(page 112)

SNOWY OWL
(page 113)

SPRING AND FALL
(page 113)

SPRUCE ROOT BASKET
(page 114)

SQUARES AND STRIPS
(page 114)

STAR AND PINWHEELS
(page 115)

STAR PUZZLE
(page 115)

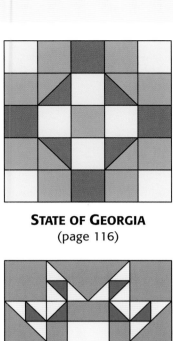

STATE OF GEORGIA
(page 116)

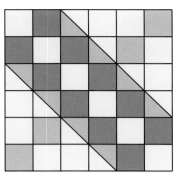

STEPPING STONES
(page 116)

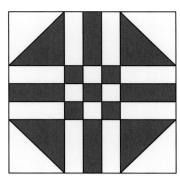

STILES AND PATHS
(page 117)

STOCKYARD'S STAR FOR NEBRASKA
(page 117)

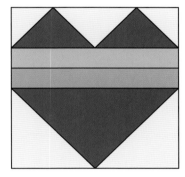

STRIP HEART
(page 118)

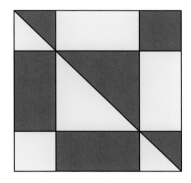

SUMMER SOLSTICE
(page 118)

SURPRISE PACKAGE
(page 119)

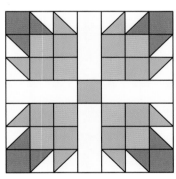

TEA ROSE
(page 119)

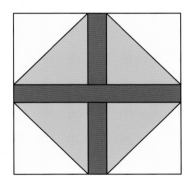

TEXAS PUZZLE
(page 120)

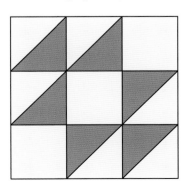

THREE AND SIX
(page 120)

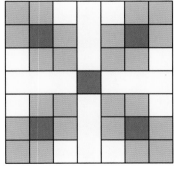

TONGANOXIE NINE PATCH
(page 121)

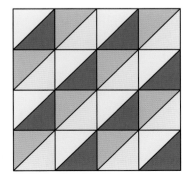

TRAIL OF TEARS
(page 121)

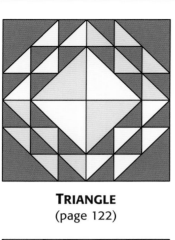

TRIANGLE
(page 122)

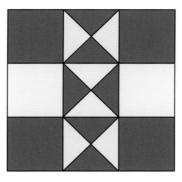

TRIPLET
(page 122)

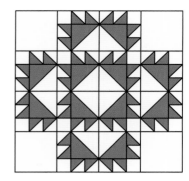

TWELVE CROWNS
(page 123)

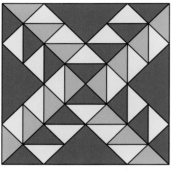

VERMONT
(page 123)

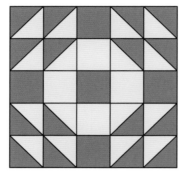

VICE PRESIDENT'S BLOCK
(page 124)

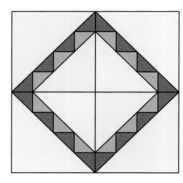

VINES AT THE WINDOW
(page 124)

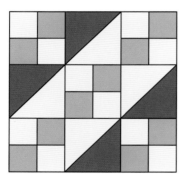

WAGON TRACKS
(page 125)

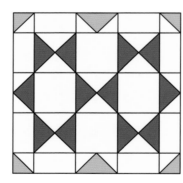

WASHINGTON STAR
(page 125)

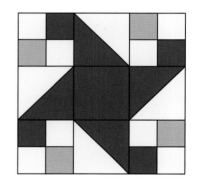

WATER WHEEL
(page 126)

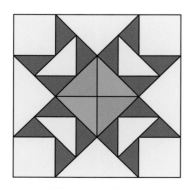

WHALES' TAILS
(page 126)

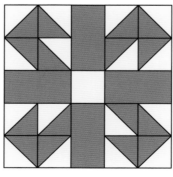

WHEEL OF CHANCE
(page 127)

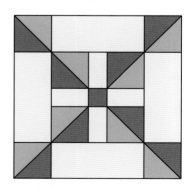

WHIRLING SQUARE
(page 127)

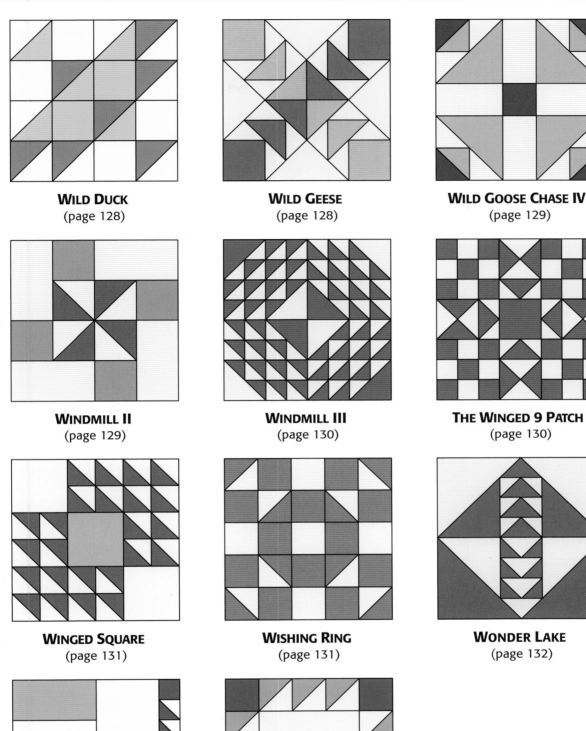

WILD DUCK
(page 128)

WILD GEESE
(page 128)

WILD GOOSE CHASE IV
(page 129)

WINDMILL II
(page 129)

WINDMILL III
(page 130)

THE WINGED 9 PATCH
(page 130)

WINGED SQUARE
(page 131)

WISHING RING
(page 131)

WONDER LAKE
(page 132)

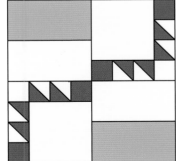

WORLD'S FAIR PUZZLE
(page 133)

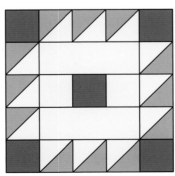

ZIGZAG
(page 133)

Block Patterns

Acrobats

5-Unit Grid

Color Illustration: page 13

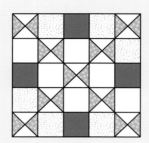 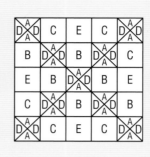 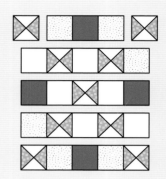

FINISHED BLOCK SIZE
Single dimensions in the cutting chart indicate the size of the cut square (3" = 3" x 3").

For 2 blocks:		5"	6¼"	7½"	8¾"	10"	12½"
Light	A: 9 ⊠→⧅	2¼"	2½"	2¾"	3"	3¼"	3¾"
	B: 12 ☐	1½"	1¾"	2"	2¼"	2½"	3"
Light 2	C: 12 ☐	1½"	1¾"	2"	2¼"	2¾"	3"
Medium	D: 9 ⊠→⧅	2¼"	2½"	2¾"	3"	3¼"	3¾"
Dark	E: 8 ☐	1½"	1¾"	2"	2¼"	2¾"	3"

Try this: Use many different mediums for D.

Alabama

9-Unit Grid

Color Illustration: page 13

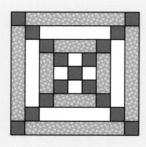 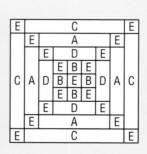 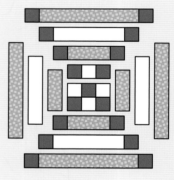

FINISHED BLOCK SIZE
Single dimensions in the cutting chart indicate the size of the cut square (3" = 3" x 3").

For 1 block:		6¾"	9"	10⅛"	11¼"	12⅜"	13½"
Light	A: 4 ☐	1¼" x 4¼"	1½" x 5½"	1⅝" x 6⅛"	1¾" x 6¾"	1⅞" x 7⅞"	2" x 8"
	B: 4 ☐	1¼"	1½"	1⅝"	1¾"	1⅞"	2"
Medium	C: 4 ☐	1¼" x 5¾"	1½" x 7½"	1⅝" x 8⅜"	1¾" x 9¼"	1⅞" x 10⅛"	2" x 11"
	D: 4 ☐	1¼" x 2¾"	1½" x 3½"	1⅝" x 3⅞"	1¾" x 4¼"	1⅞" x 4⅝"	2" x 5"
Dark	E: 17 ☐	1¼"	1½"	1⅝"	1¾"	1⅞"	2"

Try this: Use one medium for C and a different medium for D.

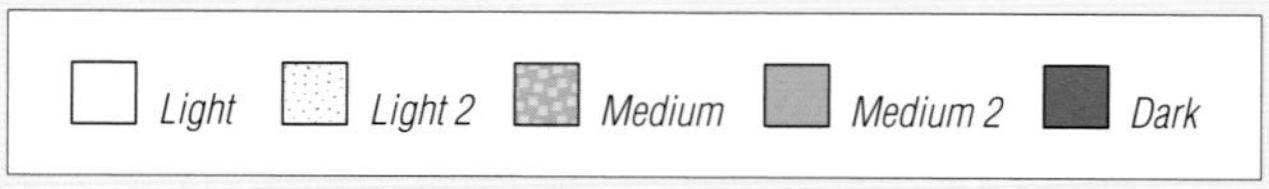

☐ Light ▨ Light 2 ▦ Medium ▨ Medium 2 ■ Dark

Album II

4-Unit Grid

Color Illustration: page 13

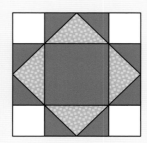
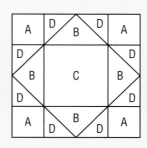
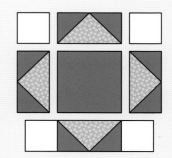

For 1 block:		FINISHED BLOCK SIZE					
		Single dimensions in the cutting chart indicate the size of the cut square (3" = 3" x 3").					
		4"	6"	8"	9"	10"	12"
Light	A: 4 ▢	1½"	2"	2½"	2¾"	3"	3½"
Medium	B: 1 ⊠→⊠	3¼"	4¼"	5¼"	5¾"	6¼"	7¼"
Dark	C: 1 ▢	2½"	3½"	4½"	5"	5½"	6½"
	D: 4 ◨→◺	1⅞"	2⅜"	2⅞"	3⅛"	3⅜"	3⅞"

Try this: Use a different combination of darks and mediums in every block.

Album III

5-Unit Grid

Color Illustration: page 13

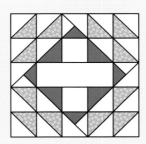
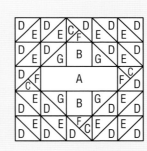
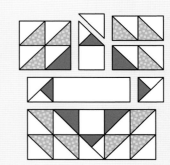

For 1 block:		FINISHED BLOCK SIZE					
		Single dimensions in the cutting chart indicate the size of the cut square (3" = 3" x 3")					
		5"	6¼"	7½"	8¾"	10"	12½"
Light	A: 1 ▭	1½" x 3½"	1¾" x 4¼"	2" x 5"	2¼" x 5¾"	2½" x 6½"	3" x 8"
	B: 2 ▢	1½"	1¾"	2"	2¼"	2½"	3"
	C: 1 ⊠→⊠	2¼"	2½"	2¾"	3"	3¼"	3¾"
	D: 10 ◨→◺	1⅞"	2⅛"	2⅜"	2⅝"	2⅞"	3⅜"
Medium	E: 6 ◨→◺	1⅞"	2⅛"	2⅜"	2⅝"	2⅞"	3⅜"
Dark	F: 1 ⊠→⊠	2¼"	2½"	2¾"	3"	3¼"	3¾"
	G: 2 ◨→◺	1⅞"	2⅛"	2⅜"	2⅝"	2⅞"	3⅜"

Try this: Use several different mediums for E.

▢ Square(s) ◨→◺ Square(s) cut once diagonally to make half-square triangles ⊠→⊠ Square(s) cut twice diagonally to make quarter-square triangles ▭ Rectangle(s)

Alpine Cross

5-Unit Grid

Color Illustration: page 13

Note: *This block is identical to Wheel of Chance (page 127) in size, shape, and position of the pieces, but the value arrangement is different.*

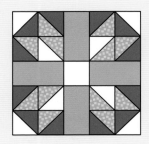
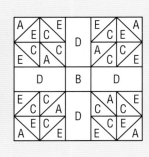
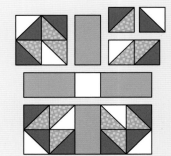

		FINISHED BLOCK SIZE					
		Single dimensions in the cutting chart indicate the size of the cut square (3" = 3" x 3").					
For 1 block:		5"	6¼"	7½"	8¾"	10"	12½"
Light	A: 4	1⅞"	2⅛"	2⅜"	2⅝"	2⅞"	3⅜"
	B: 1	1½"	1¾"	2"	2¼"	2½"	3"
Medium	C: 6	1⅞"	2⅛"	2⅜"	2⅝"	2⅞"	3⅜"
Medium 2	D: 4	1½" x 2½"	1¾" x 3"	2" x 3½"	2¼" x 4"	2½" x 4½"	3" x 5½"
Dark	E: 6	1⅞"	2⅛"	2⅜"	2⅝"	2⅞"	3⅜"

Try this: Use a different medium in every block.

Antique Tile Block

6-Unit Grid

Color Illustration: page 13

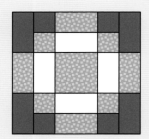
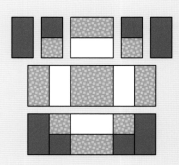

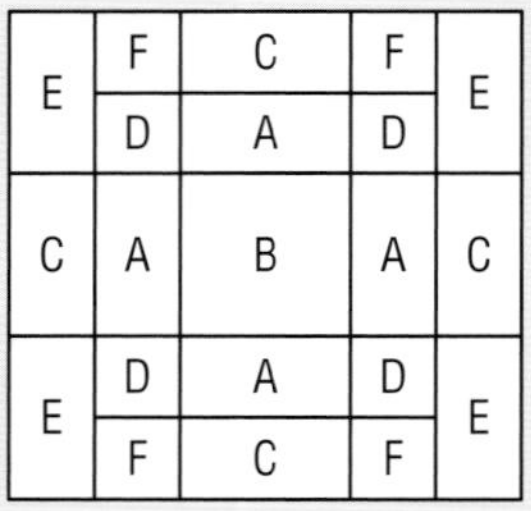

		FINISHED BLOCK SIZE					
		Single dimensions in the cutting chart indicate the size of the cut square (3" = 3" x 3").					
For 1 block:		4½"	6"	7½"	9"	10½"	12"
Light	A: 4	1¼" x 2"	1½" x 2½"	1¾" x 3"	2" x 3½"	2¼" x 4"	2½" x 4½"
Medium	B: 1	2"	2½"	3"	3½"	4"	4½"
	C: 4	1¼" x 2"	1½" x 2½"	1¾" x 3"	2" x 3½"	2¼" x 4"	2½" x 4½"
	D: 4	1¼"	1½"	1¾"	2"	2¼"	2½"
Dark	E: 4	1¼" x 2"	1½" x 2½"	1¾" x 3"	2" x 3½"	2¼" x 4"	2½" x 4½"
	F: 4	1¼"	1½"	1¾"	2"	2¼"	2½"

Try this: Use one medium for B and C and a different medium for D.

The Anvil

4-Unit Grid

Color Illustration: page 13

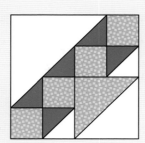 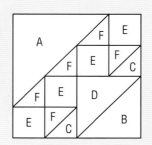 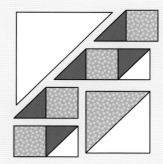

			FINISHED BLOCK SIZE					
			Single dimensions in the cutting chart indicate the size of the cut square (3" = 3" x 3").					
For 2 blocks:			4"	6"	8"	9"	10"	12"
Light	A: 1 ◻→◺		3⅞"	5⅜"	6⅞"	7⅝"	8⅜"	9⅞"
	B: 1 ◻→◺		2⅞"	3⅞"	4⅞"	5⅜"	5⅞"	6⅞"
	C: 2 ◻→◺		1⅞"	2⅜"	2⅞"	3⅛"	3⅜"	3⅞"
Medium	D: 1 ◻→◺		2⅞"	3⅞"	4⅞"	5⅜"	5⅞"	6⅞"
	E: 8 ◻		1½"	2"	2½"	2¾"	3"	3½"
Dark	F: 5 ◻→◺		1⅞"	2⅜"	2⅞"	3⅛"	3⅜"	3⅞"

Try this: Use a different medium in every block.

Arctic Nights

8-Unit Grid

Color Illustration: page 13

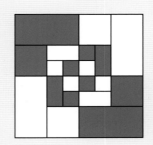 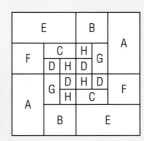 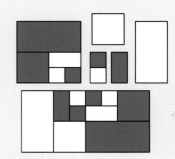

			FINISHED BLOCK SIZE					
			Single dimensions in the cutting chart indicate the size of the cut square (3" = 3" x 3").					
For 1 block:			6"	8"	9"	10"	12"	14"
Light	A: 2 ▭		2" x 3½"	2½" x 4½"	2¾" x 5"	3" x 5½"	3½" x 6½"	4" x 7½"
	B: 2 ◻		2"	2½"	2¾"	3"	3½"	4"
	C: 2 ▭		1¼" x 2"	1½" x 2½"	1⅝" x 2¾"	1¾" x 3"	2" x 3½"	2¼" x 4"
	D: 4 ◻		1¼"	1½"	1⅝"	1¾"	2"	2¼"
Dark	E: 2 ▭		2" x 3½"	2½" x 4½"	2¾" x 5"	3" x 5½"	3½" x 6½"	4" x 7½"
	F: 2 ◻		2"	2½"	2¾"	3"	3½"	4"
	G: 2 ▭		1¼" x 2"	1½" x 2½"	1⅝" x 2¾"	1¾" x 3"	2" x 3½"	2¼" x 4"
	H: 4 ◻		1¼"	1½"	1⅝"	1¾"	2"	2¼"

Try this: Use a different combination of lights and darks in each quadrant of the block.

◻ *Square(s)* ◻→◺ *Square(s) cut once diagonally to make half-square triangles* ⊠→⧖ *Square(s) cut twice diagonally to make quarter-square triangles* ▭ *Rectangle(s)*

Around the Block

5-Unit Grid

Color Illustration: page 13

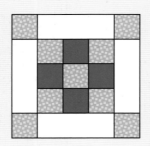

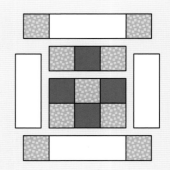

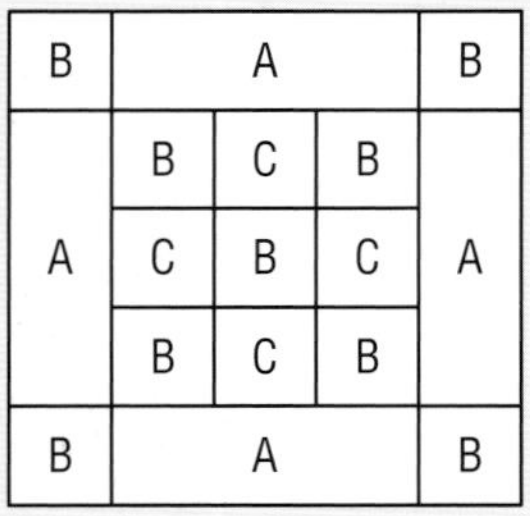

		FINISHED BLOCK SIZE					
		Single dimensions in the cutting chart indicate the size of the cut square (3" = 3" x 3").					
For 1 block:		5"	6¼"	7½"	8¾"	10"	12½"
Light	A: 4 ▢	1½" x 3½"	1¾" x 4¼"	2" x 5"	2¼" x 5¾"	2½" x 6½"	3" x 8"
Medium	B: 9 ▢	1½"	1¾"	2"	2¼"	2½"	3"
Dark	C: 4 ▢	1½"	1¾"	2"	2¼"	2½"	3"
Try this:	Use a different dark in every block.						

Aunt Kate's Choice

5-Unit Grid

Color Illustration: page 14

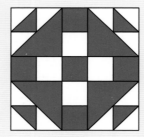

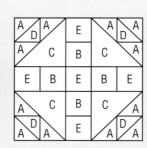

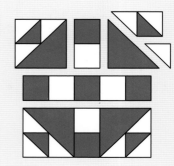

		FINISHED BLOCK SIZE					
		Single dimensions in the cutting chart indicate the size of the cut square (3" = 3" x 3").					
For 1 block:		5"	6¼"	7½"	8¾"	10"	12½"
Light	A: 6 ◱→◲	1⅞"	2⅛"	2⅜"	2⅝"	2⅞"	3⅜"
	B: 4 ▢	1½"	1¾"	2"	2¼"	2½"	3"
Dark	C: 2 ◱→◲	2⅞"	3⅜"	3⅞"	4⅜"	4⅞"	5⅞"
	D: 2 ◱→◲	1⅞"	2⅛"	2⅜"	2⅝"	2⅞"	3⅜"
	E: 5 ▢	1½"	1¾"	2"	2¼"	2½"	3"
Try this:	Use a medium instead of a dark for C.						

☐ Light ▨ Light 2 ▨ Medium ▨ Medium 2 ■ Dark

Aunt Rachel's Star

12-Unit Grid

Color Illustration: page 14

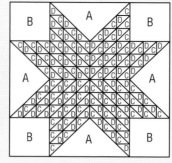

For 1 block:		FINISHED BLOCK SIZE					
		Single dimensions in the cutting chart indicate the size of the cut square (3" = 3" x 3").					
		6"	7½"	9"	12"	13½"	15"
Light	A: 1 ⊠→⊠	4¼"	5"	5¾"	7¼"	8"	8¾"
	B: 4 ☐	2"	2⅜"	2¾"	3½"	3⅞"	4¼"
	C: 36 ◺→◺	1⅜"	1½"	1⅝"	1⅞"	2"	2⅛"
Dark	D: 36 ◺→◺	1⅜"	1½"	1⅝"	1⅞"	2"	2⅛"

Try this: Use many different darks for D.

Aunt Ruth's Fancy

7-Unit Grid

Color Illustration: page 14

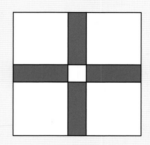
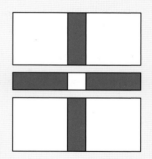

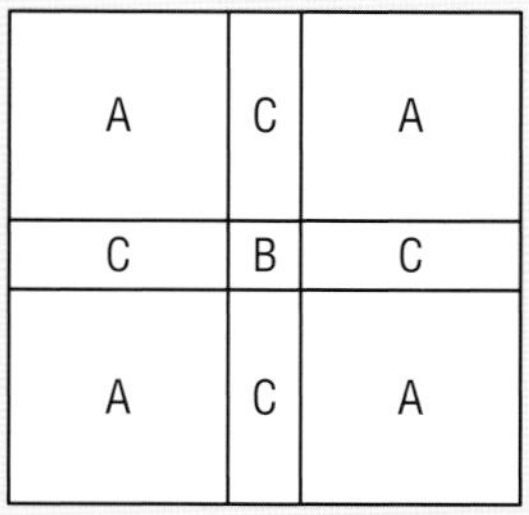

For 1 block:		FINISHED BLOCK SIZE					
		Single dimensions in the cutting chart indicate the size of the cut square (3" = 3" x 3").					
		5¼"	7"	8¾"	10½"	12¼"	14"
Light	A: 4 ☐	2¾"	3½"	4¼"	5"	5¾"	6½"
	B: 1 ☐	1¼"	1½"	1¾"	2"	2¼"	2½"
Dark	C: 4 ☐	1¼" x 2¾"	1½" x 3½"	1¾" x 4¼"	2" x 5"	2¼" x 5¾"	2½" x 6½"

Try this: Reverse the lights and darks.

☐ *Square(s)* ◸→◺ *Square(s) cut once diagonally to make half-square triangles* ⊠→⊠ *Square(s) cut twice diagonally to make quarter-square triangles* ▭ *Rectangle(s)*

Baby Bunting

4-Unit Grid

Color Illustration: page 14

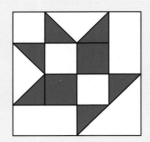 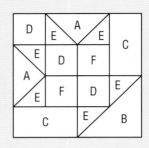 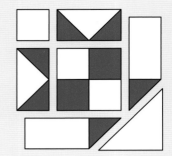

		FINISHED BLOCK SIZE					
		Single dimensions in the cutting chart indicate the size of the cut square (3" = 3" x 3").					
For 2 blocks:		4"	6"	8"	9"	10"	12"
Light	A: 1 ⊠→⊠	3¼"	4¼"	5¼"	5¾"	6¼"	7¼"
	B: 1 ◹→◹	2⅞"	3⅞"	4⅞"	5⅜"	5⅞"	6⅞"
	C: 4 ▭	1½" x 2½"	2" x 3½"	2½" x 4½"	2¾" x 5"	3" x 5½"	3½" x 6½"
	D: 6 ▢	1½"	2"	2½"	2¾"	3"	3½"
Dark	E: 6 ◹→◹	1⅞"	2⅜"	2⅞"	3⅛"	3⅜"	3⅞"
	F: 4 ▢	1½"	2"	2½"	2¾"	3"	3½"

Try this: Reverse the lights and darks in every other block.

Basket II

4-Unit Grid

Color Illustration: page 14

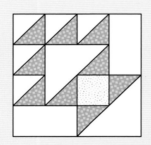 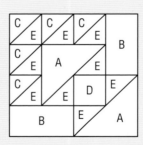 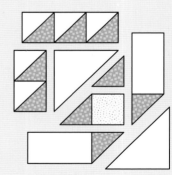

		FINISHED BLOCK SIZE					
		Single dimensions in the cutting chart indicate the size of the cut square (3" = 3" x 3").					
For 2 blocks:		4"	6"	8"	9"	10"	12"
Light	A: 2 ◹→◹	2⅞"	3⅞"	4⅞"	5⅜"	5⅞"	6⅞"
	B: 4 ▭	1½" x 2½"	2" x 3½"	2½" x 4½"	2¾" x 5"	3" x 5½"	3½" x 6½"
	C: 5 ◹→◹	1⅞"	2⅜"	2⅞"	3⅛"	3⅜"	3⅞"
Light 2	D: 2 ▢	1½"	2"	2½"	2¾"	3"	3½"
Medium	E: 9 ◹→◹	1⅞"	2⅜"	2⅞"	3⅛"	3⅜"	3⅞"

Try this: Use a dark instead of light 2 for D.

□ Light　⬚ Light 2　▨ Medium　▨ Medium 2　■ Dark

Basket of Tulips

8-Unit Grid

Color Illustration:
page 14

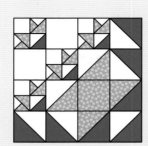
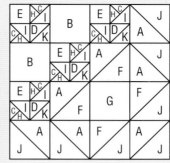
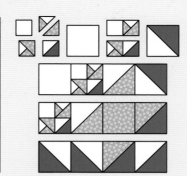

		FINISHED BLOCK SIZE
		Single dimensions in the cutting chart indicate the size of the cut square (3" = 3" x 3").

For 2 blocks:			6"	8"	9"	10"	12"	14"
Light	A: 7		2⅜"	2⅞"	3⅛"	3⅜"	3⅞"	4⅜"
	B: 4		2"	2½"	2¾"	3"	3½"	4"
	C: 4		2"	2¼"	2⅜"	2½"	2¾"	3"
	D: 4		1⅝"	1⅞"	2"	2⅛"	2⅜"	2⅝"
	E: 8		1¼"	1½"	1⅝"	1¾"	2"	2¼"
Medium	F: 4		2⅜"	2⅞"	3⅛"	3⅜"	3⅞"	4⅜"
	G: 2		2"	2½"	2¾"	3"	3½"	4"
	H: 4		2"	2¼"	2⅜"	2½"	2¾"	3"
	I: 8		1⅝"	1⅞"	2"	2⅛"	2⅜"	2⅝"
Dark	J: 7		2⅜"	2⅞"	3⅛"	3⅜"	3⅞"	4⅜"
	K: 4		1⅝"	1⅞"	2"	2⅛"	2⅜"	2⅝"

Try this: Reverse the mediums and darks.

☐ *Square(s)* ◫→◺ *Square(s) cut once diagonally to make half-square triangles* ⊠→⊠ *Square(s) cut twice diagonally to make quarter-square triangles* ▭ *Rectangle(s)*

Baton Rouge Square

5-Unit Grid

Color Illustration: page 14

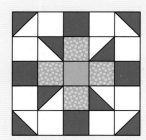
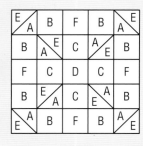
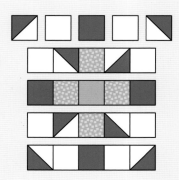

			FINISHED BLOCK SIZE					
			Single dimensions in the cutting chart indicate the size of the cut square (3" = 3" x 3").					
For 1 block:			5"	6¼"	7½"	8¾"	10"	12½"
Light	A: 4		1⅞"	2⅛"	2⅜"	2⅝"	2⅞"	3⅜"
	B: 8		1½"	1¾"	2"	2¼"	2½"	3"
Medium	C: 4		1½"	1¾"	2"	2¼"	2½"	3"
Medium 2	D: 1		1½"	1¾"	2"	2¼"	2½"	3"
Dark	E: 4		1⅞"	2⅛"	2⅜"	2⅝"	2⅞"	3⅜"
	F: 4		1½"	1¾"	2"	2¼"	2½"	3"

Try this: Use one dark for E and a different dark for F.

Berry Patch

6-Unit Grid

Color Illustration: page 14

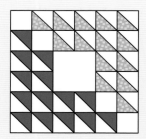
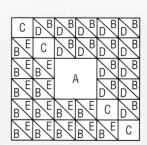
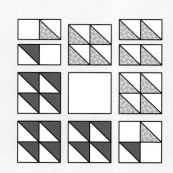

			FINISHED BLOCK SIZE					
			Single dimensions in the cutting chart indicate the size of the cut square (3" = 3" x 3").					
For 1 block:			4½"	6"	7½"	9"	10½"	12"
Light	A: 1		2"	2½"	3"	3½"	4"	4½"
	B: 14		1⅝"	1⅞"	2⅛"	2⅜"	2⅝"	2⅞"
	C: 4		1¼"	1½"	1¾"	2"	2¼"	2½"
Medium	D: 7		1⅝"	1⅞"	2⅛"	2⅜"	2⅝"	2⅞"
Dark	E: 7		1⅝"	1⅞"	2⅛"	2⅜"	2⅝"	2⅞"

Try this: Use many different mediums and darks.

☐ Light ▨ Light 2 ▦ Medium ▨ Medium 2 ■ Dark

Birch Branches

10-Unit Grid

Color Illustration: page 14

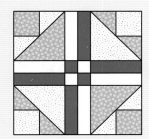
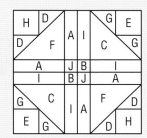
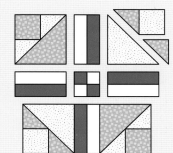

		FINISHED BLOCK SIZE					
		Single dimensions in the cutting chart indicate the size of the cut square (3" = 3" x 3").					
For 1 block:		6¼"	7½"	8¾"	10"	12½"	13¾"
Light	A: 4 ▭	1⅛" x 3"	1¼" x 3½"	1⅜" x 4"	1½" x 4½"	1¾" x 5½"	1⅞" x 6"
	B: 2 ◻	1⅛"	1¼"	1⅜"	1½"	1¾"	1⅞"
Light 2	C: 1 ◳→◺	3⅜"	3⅞"	4⅜"	4⅞"	5⅞"	6⅜"
	D: 2 ◳→◺	2⅛"	2⅜"	2⅝"	2⅞"	3⅜"	3⅝"
	E: 2 ◻	1¾"	2"	2¼"	2½"	3"	3¼"
Medium	F: 1 ◳→◺	3⅜"	3⅞"	4⅜"	4⅞"	5⅞"	6⅜"
	G: 2 ◳→◺	2⅛"	2⅜"	2⅝"	2⅞"	3⅜"	3⅝"
	H: 2 ◻	1¾"	2"	2¼"	2½"	3"	3¼"
Dark	I: 4 ▭	1⅛" x 3"	1¼" x 3½"	1⅜" x 4"	1½" x 4½"	1¾" x 5½"	1⅞" x 6"
	J: 2 ◻	1⅛"	1¼"	1⅜"	1½"	1¾"	1⅞"

Try this: Use a different combination of fabrics in each quadrant of the block.

◻ *Square(s)*   ◳→◺ *Square(s) cut once diagonally to make half-square triangles*   ⊠→ *Square(s) cut twice diagonally to make quarter-square triangles*   ▭ *Rectangle(s)*

Birds in Air

7-Unit Grid

Color Illustration: page 14

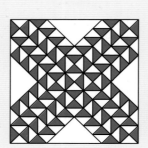
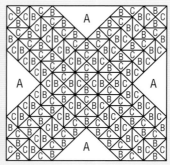

	FINISHED BLOCK SIZE					
	Single dimensions in the cutting chart indicate the size of the cut square (3" = 3" x 3").					
For 1 block:	5¼"	7"	8¾"	10½"	12¼"	14"
Light A: 1	3½"	4¼"	5"	5¾"	6½"	7¼"
B: 20	2"	2¼"	2½"	2¾"	3"	3¼"
Dark C: 20	2"	2¼"	2½"	2¾"	3"	3¼"

Try this: Reverse the darks and lights in every other block.

Birthday Cake

5-Unit Grid

Color Illustration: page 14

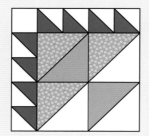
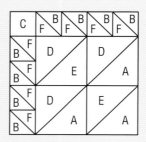
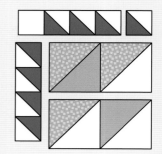

	FINISHED BLOCK SIZE					
	Single dimensions in the cutting chart indicate the size of the cut square (3" = 3" x 3")					
For 2 blocks:	5"	6¼"	7½"	8¾"	10"	12½"
Light A: 3	2⅞"	3⅜"	3⅞"	4⅜"	4⅞"	5⅞"
B: 8	1⅞"	2⅛"	2⅜"	2⅝"	2⅞"	3⅜"
C: 2	1½"	1¾"	2"	2¼"	2½"	3"
Medium D: 3	2⅞"	3⅜"	3⅞"	4⅜"	4⅞"	5⅞"
Medium 2 E: 2	2⅞"	3⅜"	3⅞"	4⅜"	4⅞"	5⅞"
Dark F: 8	1⅞"	2⅛"	2⅜"	2⅝"	2⅞"	3⅜"

Try this: Use a different medium in every block.

☐ *Light*   ▦ *Light 2*   ▨ *Medium*   ▨ *Medium 2*   ■ *Dark*

Black Labs

4-Unit Grid

Color Illustration: page 14

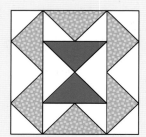
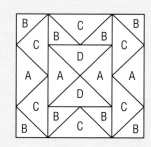

For 2 blocks:			FINISHED BLOCK SIZE Single dimensions in the cutting chart indicate the size of the cut square (3" = 3" x 3").					
			4"	**6"**	**8"**	**9"**	**10"**	**12"**
Light	A: 2	⊠→⊠	3¼"	4¼"	5¼"	5¾"	6¼"	7¼"
	B: 8	◻→◸	1⅞"	2⅜"	2⅞"	3⅛"	3⅜"	3⅞"
Medium	C: 3	⊠→⊠	3¼"	4¼"	5¼"	5¾"	6¼"	7¼"
Dark	D: 1	⊠→⊠	3¼"	4¼"	5¼"	5¾"	6¼"	7¼"

Try this: Reverse the lights and mediums in every other block.

Black Spruce

6-Unit Grid

Color Illustration: page 15

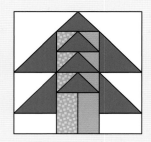
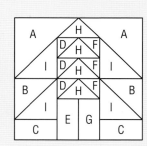
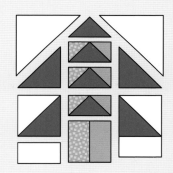

For 2 blocks:			FINISHED BLOCK SIZE Single dimensions in the cutting chart indicate the size of the cut square (3" = 3" x 3").					
			4½"	**6"**	**7½"**	**9"**	**10½"**	**12"**
Light	A: 2	◻→◺	3⅛"	3⅞"	4⅝"	5⅜"	6⅛"	6⅞"
	B: 2	◻→◺	2⅜"	2⅞"	3⅜"	3⅞"	4⅜"	4⅞"
	C: 4	▭	1¼" x 2"	1½" x 2½"	1¾" x 3"	2" x 3½"	2¼" x 4"	2½" x 4½"
Medium	D: 3	◻→◺	1⅝"	1⅞"	2⅛"	2⅜"	2⅝"	2⅞"
	E: 2	▭	1¼" x 2"	1½" x 2½"	1¾" x 3"	2" x 3½"	2¼" x 4"	2½" x 4½"
Medium 2	F: 3	◻→◺	1⅝"	1⅞"	2⅛"	2⅜"	2⅝"	2⅞"
	G: 2	▭	1¼" x 2"	1½" x 2½"	1¾" x 3"	2" x 3½"	2¼" x 4"	2½" x 4½"
Dark	H: 2	⊠→⊠	2¾"	3¼"	3¾"	4¼"	4¾"	5¼"
	I: 4	◻→◺	2⅜"	2⅞"	3⅜"	3⅞"	4⅜"	4⅞"

Try this: Use one dark for H and a different dark for I.

◻ Square(s)   ◻→◺ Square(s) cut once diagonally to make half-square triangles   ⊠→⊠ Square(s) cut twice diagonally to make quarter-square triangles   ▭ Rectangle(s)

Blazed Trail

8-Unit Grid

Color Illustration: page 15

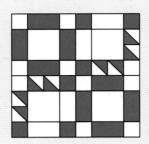
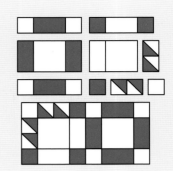
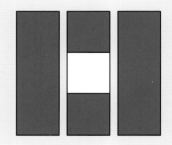

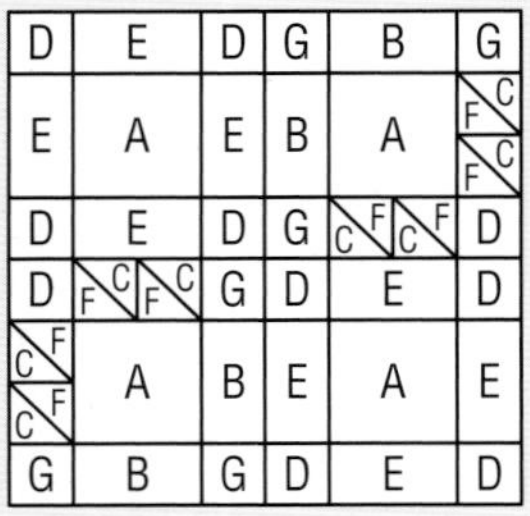

		FINISHED BLOCK SIZE					
		Single dimensions in the cutting chart indicate the size of the cut square (3" = 3" x 3").					
For 1 block:		6"	8"	9"	10"	12"	14"
Light	A: 4 ▢	2"	2½"	2¾"	3"	3½"	4"
	B: 4 ▭	1¼" x 2"	1½" x 2½"	1⅝" x 2¾"	1¾" x 3"	2" x 3½"	2¼" x 4"
	C: 4 ◧→◩	1⅝"	1⅞"	2"	2⅛"	2⅜"	2⅝"
	D: 10 ▢	1¼"	1½"	1⅝"	1¾"	2"	2¼"
Dark	E: 8 ▭	1¼" x 2"	1½" x 2½"	1⅝" x 2¾"	1¾" x 3"	2" x 3½"	2¼" x 4"
	F: 4 ◧→◩	1⅝"	1⅞"	2"	2⅛"	2⅜"	2⅝"
	G: 6 ▢	1¼"	1½"	1⅝"	1¾"	2"	2¼"

Try this: Use a medium instead of a light for A.

Blocks in a Box

3-Unit Grid

Color Illustration: page 15

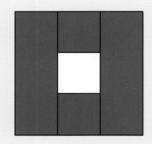
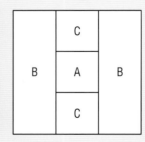
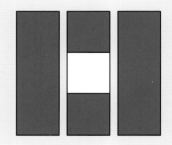

		FINISHED BLOCK SIZE					
		Single dimensions in the cutting chart indicate the size of the cut square (3" = 3" x 3").					
For 1 block:		4½"	6"	7½"	9"	10½"	12"
Light	A: 1 ▢	2"	2½"	3"	3½"	4"	4½"
Dark	B: 2 ▭	2" x 5"	2½" x 6½"	3" x 8"	3½" x 9½"	4" x 11"	4½" x 12½"
	C: 2 ▢	2"	2½"	3"	3½"	4"	4½"

Try this: Use a medium instead of a dark in every other block.

Blue Fields

8-Unit Grid

Color Illustration: page 15

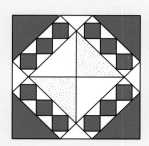 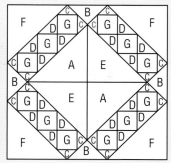 

For 1 block:			FINISHED BLOCK SIZE					
			Single dimensions in the cutting chart indicate the size of the cut square (3" = 3" x 3").					
			6"	8"	9"	10"	12"	14"
Light	A: 1		3⅛"	3⅞"	4¼"	4⅝"	5⅜"	6⅛"
	B: 1		2¾"	3¼"	3½"	3¾"	4¼"	4¾"
	C: 4		2"	2¼"	2⅜"	2½"	2¾"	3"
	D: 8		1⅝"	1⅞"	2"	2⅛"	2⅜"	2⅝"
Light 2	E: 1		3⅛"	3⅞"	4¼"	4⅝"	5⅜"	6⅛"
Dark	F: 2		3⅛"	3⅞"	4¼"	4⅝"	5⅜"	6⅛"
	G: 12		1¼"	1½"	1⅝"	1¾"	2"	2¼"

Try this: Use several different darks for G.

	Square(s)		Square(s) cut once diagonally to make half-square triangles		Square(s) cut twice diagonally to make quarter-square triangles		Rectangle(s)

Blue Grouse

10-Unit Grid

Color Illustration: page 15

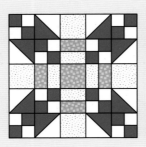
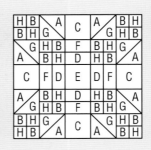
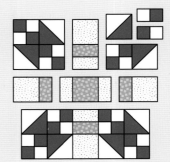

FINISHED BLOCK SIZE						
Single dimensions in the cutting chart indicate the size of the cut square (3" = 3" x 3").						

For 1 block:			6¼"	7½"	8¾"	10"	12½"	13¾"
Light	A: 4 ▢→◪		2⅛"	2⅜"	2⅝"	2⅞"	3⅜"	3⅝"
	B: 16 ▢		1⅛"	1¼"	1⅜"	1½"	1¾"	1⅞"
Light 2	C: 4 ▢		1¾"	2"	2¼"	2½"	3"	3¼"
	D: 4 ▭		1⅛" x 1¾"	1¼" x 2"	1⅜" x 2¼"	1½" x 2½"	1¾" x 3"	1⅞" x 3¼"
Medium	E: 1 ▢		1¾"	2"	2¼"	2½"	3"	3¼"
	F: 4 ▭		1⅛" x 1¾"	1¼" x 2"	1⅜" x 2¼"	1½" x 2½"	1¾" x 3"	1⅞" x 3¼"
Dark	G: 4 ▢→◪		2⅛"	2⅜"	2⅝"	2⅞"	3⅜"	3⅝"
	H: 16 ▢		1⅛"	1¼"	1⅜"	1½"	1¾"	1⅞"

Try this: Use one dark for G and a different dark for H.

☐ Light ▨ Light 2 ▦ Medium ▩ Medium 2 ■ Dark

Blueberry Buckle

10-Unit Grid

Color Illustration: page 15

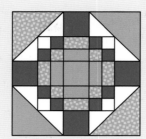 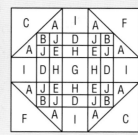 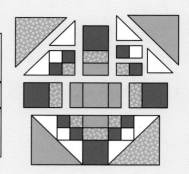

		FINISHED BLOCK SIZE					
		Single dimensions in the cutting chart indicate the size of the cut square (3" = 3" x 3").					
For 1 block:		6¼"	7½"	8¾"	10"	12½"	13¾"
Light	A: 4 ◻→◨	2⅛"	2⅜"	2⅝"	2⅞"	3⅜"	3⅝"
	B: 4 ◻	1⅛"	1¼"	1⅜"	1½"	1¾"	1⅞"
Medium	C: 1 ◻→◨	3⅜"	3⅞"	4⅜"	4⅞"	5⅞"	6⅜"
	D: 4 ▭	1⅛" x 1¾"	1¼" x 2"	1⅜" x 2¼"	1½" x 2½"	1¾" x 3"	1⅞" x 3¼"
	E: 4 ◻	1⅛"	1¼"	1⅜"	1½"	1¾"	1⅞"
Medium 2	F: 1 ◻→◨	3⅜"	3⅞"	4⅜"	4⅞"	5⅞"	6⅜"
	G: 1 ◻	1¾"	2"	2¼"	2½"	3"	3¼"
	H: 4 ▭	1⅛" x 1¾"	1¼" x 2"	1⅜" x 2¼"	1½" x 2½"	1¾" x 3"	1⅞" x 3¼"
Dark	I: 4 ◻	1¾"	2"	2¼"	2½"	3"	3¼"
	J: 8 ◻	1⅛"	1¼"	1⅜"	1½"	1¾"	1⅞"

Try this: Use a dark instead of medium 2 for G.

◻ Square(s)	◸→◨ Square(s) cut once diagonally to make half-square triangles	⊠→⊠ Square(s) cut twice diagonally to make quarter-square triangles	▭ Rectangle(s)

Boxed In

5-Unit Grid

Color Illustration: page 15

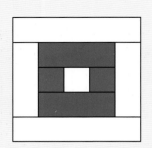 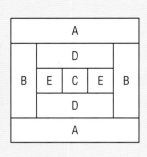 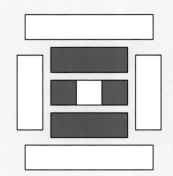

For 1 block:		FINISHED BLOCK SIZE					
		Single dimensions in the cutting chart indicate the size of the cut square (3" = 3" x 3").					
		5"	6¼"	7½"	8¾"	10"	12½"
Light	A: 2 ☐	1½" x 5½"	1¾" x 6¾"	2" x 8"	2¼" x 9¼"	2½" x 10½"	3" x 13"
	B: 2 ☐	1½" x 3½"	1¾" x 4¼"	2" x 5"	2¼" x 5¾"	2½" x 6½"	3" x 8"
	C: 1 ☐	1½"	1¾"	2"	2¼"	2½"	3"
Dark	D: 2 ☐	1½" x 3½"	1¾" x 4¼"	2" x 5"	2¼" x 5¾"	2½" x 6½"	3" x 8"
	E: 2 ☐	1½"	1¾"	2"	2¼"	2½"	3"

Try this: Reverse the lights and darks in every other block.

Building Blocks

5-Unit Grid

Color Illustration: page 15

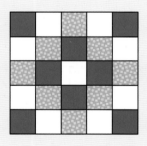 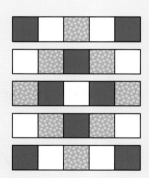

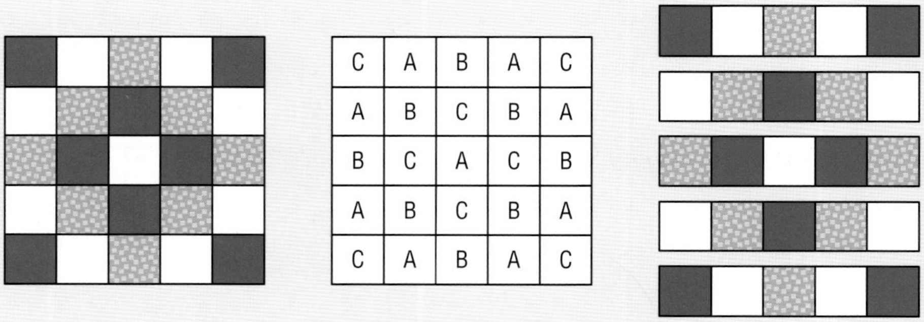

For 1 block:		FINISHED BLOCK SIZE					
		Single dimensions in the cutting chart indicate the size of the cut square (3" = 3" x 3").					
		5"	6¼"	7½"	8¾"	10"	12½"
Light	A: 9 ☐	1½"	1¾"	2"	2¼"	2½"	3"
Medium	B: 8 ☐	1½"	1¾"	2"	2¼"	2½"	3"
Dark	C: 8 ☐	1½"	1¾"	2"	2¼"	2½"	3"

Try this: Use several different lights for A.

☐ Light   ☐ Light 2   ☐ Medium   ☐ Medium 2   ☐ Dark

Building Blocks II

9-Unit Grid

Color Illustration: page 15

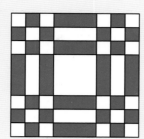

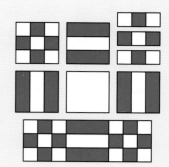

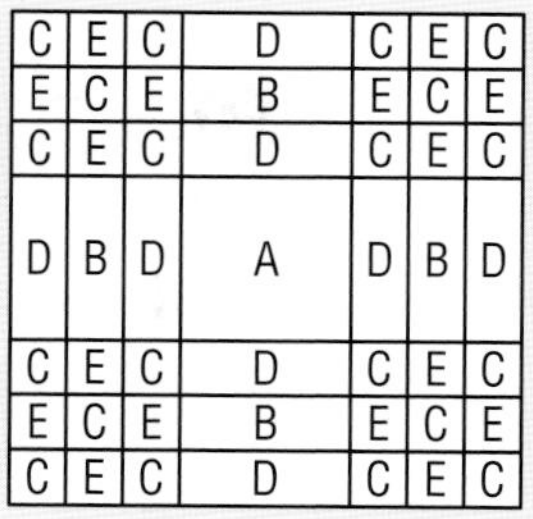

C	E	C	D	C	E	C

(diagram grid with labels C E C D C E C / E C E B E C E / C E C D C E C / D B D A D B D / C E C D C E C / E C E B E C E / C E C D C E C)

	FINISHED BLOCK SIZE					
	Single dimensions in the cutting chart indicate the size of the cut square (3" = 3" x 3").					
For 1 block:	6¾"	9"	10⅛"	11¼"	12⅜"	13½"
Light A: 1 ▢	2¾"	3½"	3⅞"	4¼"	4⅝"	5"
B: 4 ▭	1¼" x 2¾"	1½" x 3½"	1⅝" x 3⅞"	1¾" x 4¼"	1⅞" x 4⅝"	2" x 5"
C: 20 ▢	1¼"	1½"	1⅝"	1¾"	1⅞"	2"
Dark D: 8 ▭	1¼" x 2¾"	1½" x 3½"	1⅝" x 3⅞"	1¾" x 4¼"	1⅞" x 4⅝"	2" x 5"
E: 16 ▢	1¼"	1½"	1⅝"	1¾"	1⅞"	2"

Try this: Use a medium instead of a light for A and B.

Cactus Pot

4-Unit Grid

Color Illustration: page 15

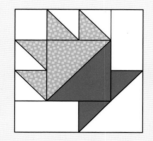

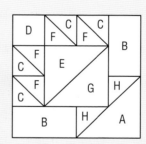

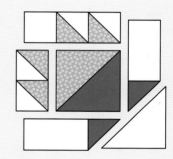

(diagram labels: D, F, C, C, F, C, E, B, F, C, F, G, H, B, H, A)

	FINISHED BLOCK SIZE					
	Single dimensions in the cutting chart indicate the size of the cut square (3" = 3" x 3").					
For 2 blocks:	4"	6"	8"	9"	10"	12"
Light A: 1 ◪	2⅞"	3⅞"	4⅞"	5⅜"	5⅞"	6⅞"
B: 4 ▭	1½" x 2½"	2" x 3½"	2½" x 4½"	2¾" x 5"	3" x 5½"	3½" x 6½"
C: 4 ◪	1⅞"	2⅜"	2⅞"	3⅛"	3⅜"	3⅞"
D: 2 ▢	1½"	2"	2½"	2¾"	3"	3½"
Medium E: 1 ◪	2⅞"	3⅞"	4⅞"	5⅜"	5⅞"	6⅞"
F: 4 ◪	1⅞"	2⅜"	2⅞"	3⅛"	3⅜"	3⅞"
Dark G: 1 ◪	2⅞"	3⅞"	4⅞"	5⅜"	5⅞"	6⅞"
H: 2 ◪	1⅞"	2⅜"	2⅞"	3⅛"	3⅜"	3⅞"

Try this: Use one medium for E and a different medium for F.

▢ Square(s)   ◪ Square(s) cut once diagonally to make half-square triangles   ⊠ Square(s) cut twice diagonally to make quarter-square triangles   ▭ Rectangle(s)

Castle Garden

8-Unit Grid

Color Illustration: page 15

 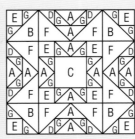 

FINISHED BLOCK SIZE						
Single dimensions in the cutting chart indicate the size of the cut square (3" = 3" x 3").						
For 1 block:		6"	8"	9"	10"	12"	14"

For 1 block:			6"	8"	9"	10"	12"	14"
Light	A: 3 ⊠→⊠		2¾"	3¼"	3½"	3¾"	4¼"	4¾"
	B: 2 ◻→◻		2⅜"	2⅞"	3⅛"	3⅜"	3⅞"	4⅜"
	C: 1 ▢		2"	2½"	2¾"	3"	3½"	4"
	D: 4 ◻→◻		1⅝"	1⅞"	2"	2⅛"	2⅜"	2⅝"
Medium	E: 8 ▢		1¼"	1½"	1⅝"	1¾"	2"	2¼"
Dark	F: 4 ◻→◻		2⅜"	2⅞"	3⅛"	3⅜"	3⅞"	4⅜"
	G: 12 ◻→◻		1⅝"	1⅞"	2"	2⅛"	2⅜"	2⅝"

Try this: Use one dark for F and a different dark for G.

Chain and Bar

8-Unit Grid

Color Illustration: page 15

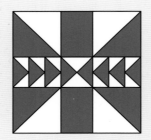 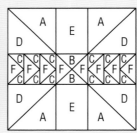 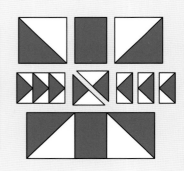

FINISHED BLOCK SIZE						
Single dimensions in the cutting chart indicate the size of the cut square (3" = 3" x 3").						

For 2 blocks:			6"	8"	9"	10"	12"	14"
Light	A: 4 ◻→◻		3⅛"	3⅞"	4¼"	4⅝"	5⅜"	6⅛"
	B: 1 ⊠→⊠		2¾"	3¼"	3½"	3¾"	4¼"	4¾"
	C: 12 ◻→◻		1⅝"	1⅞"	2"	2⅛"	2⅜"	2⅝"
Dark	D: 4 ◻→◻		3⅛"	3⅞"	4¼"	4⅝"	5⅜"	6⅛"
	E: 4 ▭		2" x 2¾"	2½" x 3½"	2¾" x 3⅞"	3" x 4¼"	3½" x 5"	4" x 5¾"
	F: 4 ⊠→⊠		2¾"	3¼"	3½"	3¾"	4¼"	4¾"

Try this: Use several different darks for F.

◻ Light   ⬚ Light 2   ▦ Medium   ▨ Medium 2   ■ Dark

Chickadee Quadrille

9-Unit Grid

Color Illustration: page 16

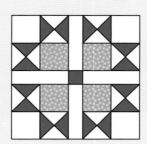
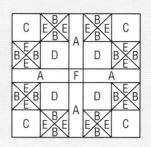
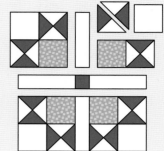

FINISHED BLOCK SIZE						
Single dimensions in the cutting chart indicate the size of the cut square (3" = 3" x 3").						
For 1 block:	6¾"	9"	10⅛"	11¼"	12⅜"	13½"
Light A: 4 ▭	1¼" x 3½"	1½" x 4½"	1⅝" x 5"	1¾" x 5½"	1⅞" x 6"	2" x 6½"
B: 4 ⊠→⊠	2¾"	3¼"	3½"	3¾"	4"	4¼"
C: 4 ▫	2"	2½"	2¾"	3"	3¼"	3½"
Medium D: 4 ▫	2"	2½"	2¾"	3"	3¼"	3½"
Dark E: 4 ⊠→⊠	2¾"	3¼"	3½"	3¾"	4"	4¼"
F: 1 ▫	1¼"	1½"	1⅝"	1¾"	1⅞"	2"

Try this: Use one light for A and a different light for B and C.

The Chinese Block Quilt

6-Unit Grid

Color Illustration: page 16

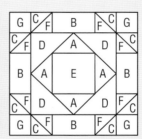

FINISHED BLOCK SIZE						
Single dimensions in the cutting chart indicate the size of the cut square (3" = 3" x 3").						
For 1 block:	4½"	6"	7½"	9"	10½"	12"
Light A: 1 ⊠→⊠	2¾"	3¼"	3¾"	4¼"	4¾"	5¼"
B: 4 ▭	1¼" x 2"	1½" x 2½"	1¾" x 3"	2" x 3½"	2¼" x 4"	2½" x 4½"
C: 4 ◸→◺	1⅝"	1⅞"	2⅛"	2⅜"	2⅝"	2⅞"
Dark D: 2 ◸→◺	2⅜"	2⅞"	3⅜"	3⅞"	4⅜"	4⅞"
E: 1 ▫	2"	2½"	3"	3½"	4"	4½"
F: 4 ◸→◺	1⅝"	1⅞"	2⅛"	2⅜"	2⅝"	2⅞"
G: 4 ▫	1¼"	1½"	1¾"	2"	2¼"	2½"

Try this: Use a medium instead of a dark for F.

▢ Square(s)   ◹→◺ Square(s) cut once diagonally to make half-square triangles   ⊠→⊠ Square(s) cut twice diagonally to make quarter-square triangles   ▭ Rectangle(s)

Chisholm Trail

4-Unit Grid

Color Illustration: page 16

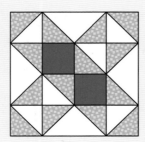
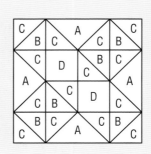
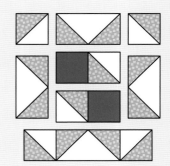

		FINISHED BLOCK SIZE					
		Single dimensions in the cutting chart indicate the size of the cut square (3" = 3" x 3").					
For 1 block:		4"	6"	8"	9"	10"	12"
Light	A: 1 ⊠ → ⊠	3¼"	4¼"	5¼"	5¾"	6¼"	7¼"
	B: 3 ◲ → ◱	1⅞"	2⅜"	2⅞"	3⅛"	3⅜"	3⅞"
Medium	C: 7 ◲ → ◱	1⅞"	2⅜"	2⅞"	3⅛"	3⅜"	3⅞"
Dark	D: 2 ☐	1½"	2"	2½"	2¾"	3"	3½"

Try this: Use several different mediums for C.

Christmas Star II

5-Unit Grid

Color Illustration: page 16

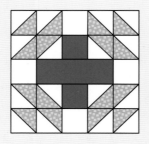
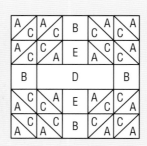
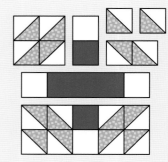

		FINISHED BLOCK SIZE					
		Single dimensions in the cutting chart indicate the size of the cut square (3" = 3" x 3").					
For 1 block:		5"	6¼"	7½"	8¾"	10"	12½"
Light	A: 8 ◲ → ◱	1⅞"	2⅛"	2⅜"	2⅝"	2⅞"	3⅜"
	B: 4 ☐	1½"	1¾"	2"	2¼"	2½"	3"
Medium	C: 8 ◲ → ◱	1⅞"	2⅛"	2⅜"	2⅝"	2⅞"	3⅜"
Dark	D: 1 ▭	1½" x 3½"	1¾" x 4¼"	2" x 5"	2¼" x 5¾"	2½" x 6½"	3" x 8"
	E: 2 ☐	1½"	1¾"	2"	2¼"	2½"	3"

Try this: Reverse the darks and mediums in every other block.

Light | Light 2 | Medium | Medium 2 | Dark

50

The Comfort Quilt

9-Unit Grid

Color Illustration: page 16

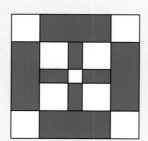

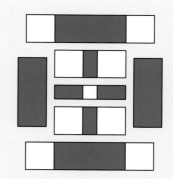

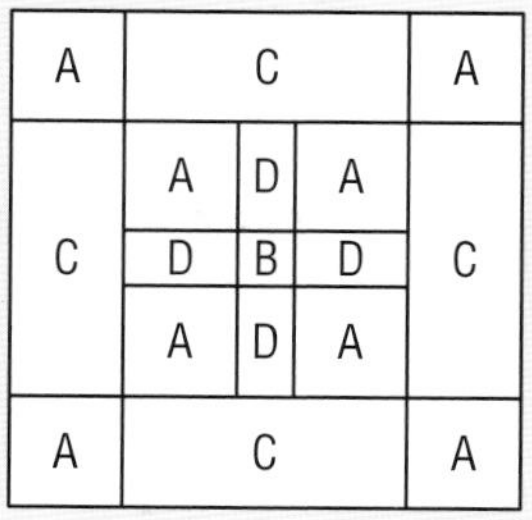

		FINISHED BLOCK SIZE					
		Single dimensions in the cutting chart indicate the size of the cut square (3" = 3" x 3").					
For 1 block:		6¾"	9"	10⅛"	11¼"	12⅜"	13½"
Light	A: 8 ▢	2"	2½"	2¾"	3"	3¼"	3½"
	B: 1 ▢	1¼"	1½"	1⅝"	1¾"	1⅞"	2"
Dark	C: 4 ▭	2" x 4¼"	2½" x 5½"	2¾" x 6⅛"	3" x 6¾"	3¼" x 7⅜"	3½" x 8"
	D: 4 ▭	1¼" x 2"	1½" x 2½"	1⅝" x 2¾"	1¾" x 3"	1⅞" x 3¼"	2" x 3½"

Try this: Use one dark for C and a different dark for D.

The Continental

9-Unit Grid

Color Illustration: page 16

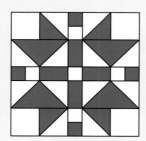

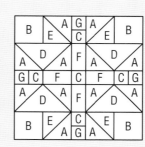

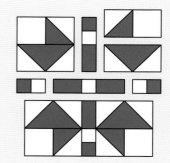

		FINISHED BLOCK SIZE					
		Single dimensions in the cutting chart indicate the size of the cut square (3" = 3" x 3").					
For 1 block:		6¾"	9"	10⅛"	11¼"	12⅜"	13½"
Light	A: 6 ◺→◺	2⅜"	2⅞"	3⅛"	3⅜"	3⅝"	3⅞"
	B: 4 ▢	2"	2½"	2¾"	3"	3¼"	3½"
	C: 5 ▢	1¼"	1½"	1⅝"	1¾"	1⅞"	2"
Dark	D: 1 ⊠→⊠	4¼"	5¼"	5¾"	6¼"	6¾"	7¼"
	E: 2 ◺→◺	2⅜"	2⅞"	3⅛"	3⅜"	3⅝"	3⅞"
	F: 4 ▭	1¼" x 2"	1½" x 2½"	1⅝" x 2¾"	1¾" x 3"	1⅞" x 3¼"	2" x 3½"
	G: 4 ▢	1¼"	1½"	1⅝"	1¾"	1⅞"	2"

Try this: Use a medium instead of a dark for F and G.

▢ Square(s)	◺→◺ Square(s) cut once diagonally to make half-square triangles	⊠→⊠ Square(s) cut twice diagonally to make quarter-square triangles	▭ Rectangle(s)

Counterchange Cross

6-Unit Grid

Color Illustration: page 16

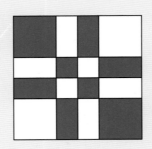

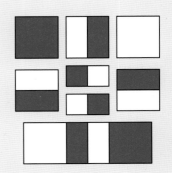

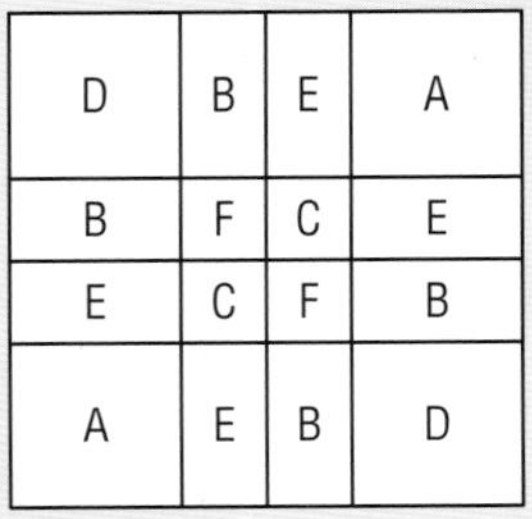

B	F	C	E
D	B	E	A
E	C	F	B
A	E	B	D

(grid shown: row1 D B E A, row2 B F C E, row3 E C F B, row4 A E B D)

FINISHED BLOCK SIZE
Single dimensions in the cutting chart indicate the size of the cut square (3" = 3" x 3").

For 1 block:			4½"	6"	7½"	9"	10½"	12"
Light	A: 2		2"	2½"	3"	3½"	4"	4½"
	B: 4		1¼" x 2"	1½" x 2½"	1¾" x 3"	2" x 3½"	2¼" x 4"	2½" x 4½"
	C: 2		1¼"	1½"	1¾"	2"	2¼"	2½"
Dark	D: 2		2"	2½"	3"	3½"	4"	4½"
	E: 4		1¼" x 2"	1½" x 2½"	1¾" x 3"	2" x 3½"	2¼" x 4"	2½" x 4½"
	F: 2		1¼"	1½"	1¾"	2"	2¼"	2½"

Try this: Use a different combination of lights and darks in each quadrant of the block.

Counterpane

6-Unit Grid

Color Illustration: page 16

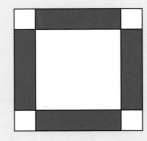

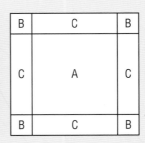

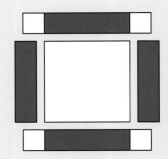

B	C	B
C	A	C
B	C	B

FINISHED BLOCK SIZE
Single dimensions in the cutting chart indicate the size of the cut square (3" = 3" x 3").

For 1 block:			4½"	6"	7½"	9"	10½"	12"
Light	A: 1		3½"	4½"	5½"	6½"	7½"	8½"
	B: 4		1¼"	1½"	1¾"	2"	2¼"	2½"
Dark	C: 4		1¼" x 3½"	1½" x 4½"	1¾" x 5½"	2" x 6½"	2¼" x 7½"	2½" x 8½"

Try this: Use a large-scale print for A.

☐ Light	⬚ Light 2	▦ Medium	▨ Medium 2	■ Dark

Country Lanes

5-Unit Grid

Color Illustration: page 16

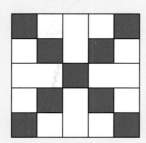

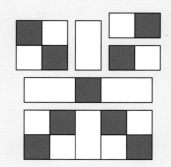

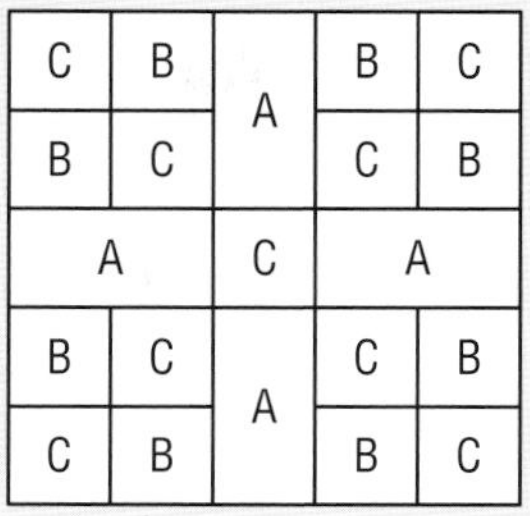

		FINISHED BLOCK SIZE					
		Single dimensions in the cutting chart indicate the size of the cut square (3" = 3" x 3").					
For 1 block:		5"	6¼"	7½"	8¾"	10"	12½"
Light	A: 4	1½" x 2½"	1¾" x 3"	2" x 3½"	2¼" x 4"	2½" x 4½"	3" x 5½"
	B: 8	1½"	1¾"	2"	2¼"	2½"	3"
Dark	C: 9	1½"	1¾"	2"	2¼"	2½"	3"

Try this: Use a medium instead of a light for A.

The Crayon Box

6-Unit Grid

Color Illustration: page 16

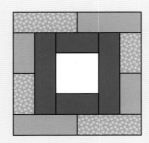

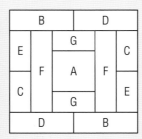

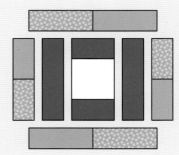

		FINISHED BLOCK SIZE					
		Single dimensions in the cutting chart indicate the size of the cut square (3" = 3" x 3").					
For 1 block:		4½"	6"	7½"	9"	10½"	12"
Light	A: 1	2"	2½"	3"	3½"	4"	4½"
Medium	B: 2	1¼" x 2¾"	1½" x 3½"	1¾" x 4¼"	2" x 5"	2¼" x 5¾"	2½" x 6½"
	C: 2	1¼" x 2"	1½" x 2½"	1¾" x 3"	2" x 3½"	2¼" x 4"	2½" x 4½"
Medium 2	D: 2	1¼" x 2¾"	1½" x 3½"	1¾" x 4¼"	2" x 5"	2¼" x 5¾"	2½" x 6½"
	E: 2	1¼" x 2"	1½" x 2½"	1¾" x 3"	2" x 3½"	2¼" x 4"	2½" x 4½"
Dark	F: 2	1¼" x 3½"	1½" x 4½"	1¾" x 5½"	2" x 6½"	2¼" x 7½"	2½" x 8½"
	G: 2	1¼" x 2"	1½" x 2½"	1¾" x 3"	2" x 3½"	2¼" x 4"	2½" x 4½"

Try this: Use a scrappy assortment of mediums for B, C, D and E.

☐ Square(s) ◺→◹ Square(s) cut once diagonally to make half-square triangles ⊠→⊠ Square(s) cut twice diagonally to make quarter-square triangles ▭ Rectangle(s)

Crazy Ann

8-Unit Grid

Color Illustration: page 16

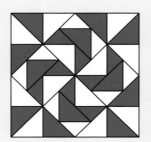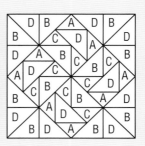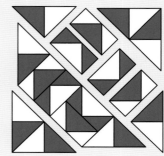

FINISHED BLOCK SIZE

Single dimensions in the cutting chart indicate the size of the cut square (3" = 3" x 3").

For 1 block:			6"	8"	9"	10"	12"	14"
Light	A: 2 ⊠→⊠		2¾"	3¼"	3½"	3¾"	4¼"	4¾"
	B: 6 ◹→◹		2⅜"	2⅞"	3⅛"	3⅜"	3⅞"	4⅜"
Dark	C: 2 ⊠→⊠		2¾"	3¼"	3½"	3¾"	4¼"	4¾"
	D: 6 ◹→◹		2⅜"	2⅞"	3⅛"	3⅜"	3⅞"	4⅜"

Try this: Reverse the lights and darks in every other block.

Cross and Crown

7-Unit Grid

Color Illustration: page 16

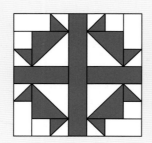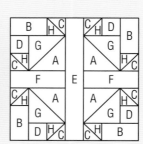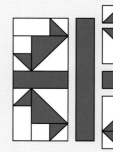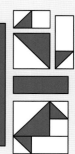

FINISHED BLOCK SIZE

Single dimensions in the cutting chart indicate the size of the cut square (3" = 3" x 3").

For 1 block:			5¼"	7"	8¾"	10½"	12¼"	14"
Light	A: 2 ◹→◹		2⅜"	2⅞"	3⅜"	3⅞"	4⅜"	4⅞"
	B: 4 ▭		1¼" x 2"	1½" x 2½"	1¾" x 3"	2" x 3½"	2¼" x 4"	2½" x 4½"
	C: 4 ◹→◹		1⅝"	1⅞"	2⅛"	2⅜"	2⅝"	2⅞"
	D: 4 ▫		1¼"	1½"	1¾"	2"	2¼"	2½"
Dark	E: 1 ▭		1¼" x 5¾"	1½" x 7½"	1¾" x 9¼"	2" x 11"	2¼" x 12¾"	2½" x 14½"
	F: 2 ▭		1¼" x 2¾"	1½" x 3½"	1¾" x 4¼"	2" x 5"	2¼" x 5¾"	2½" x 6½"
	G: 2 ◹→◹		2⅜"	2⅞"	3⅜"	3⅞"	4⅜"	4⅞"
	H: 4 ◹→◹		1⅝"	1⅞"	2⅛"	2⅜"	2⅝"	2⅞"

Try this: Use a medium instead of a dark for E and F.

□ *Light* ▦ *Light 2* ▨ *Medium* ▨ *Medium 2* ■ *Dark*

Crossroads

8-Unit Grid

Color Illustration: page 17

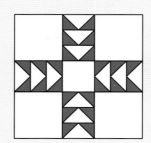 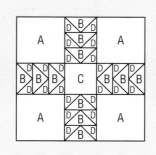

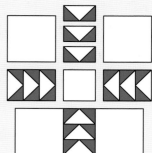

		FINISHED BLOCK SIZE					
		Single dimensions in the cutting chart indicate the size of the cut square (3" = 3" x 3").					
For 1 block:		6"	8"	9"	10"	12"	14"
Light	A: 4 ▢	2¾"	3½"	3⅞"	4¼"	5"	5¾"
	B: 3 ⊠→⊠	2¾"	3¼"	3½"	3¾"	4¼"	4¾"
	C: 1 ▢	2"	2½"	2¾"	3"	3½"	4"
Dark	D: 12 ◺→◺	1⅝"	1⅞"	2"	2⅛"	2⅜"	2⅝"

Try this: Use one light for A and C and a different light for B.

Crown and Star

8-Unit Grid

Color Illustration: page 17

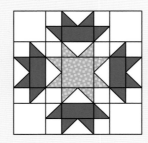 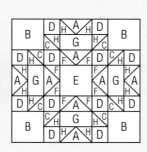

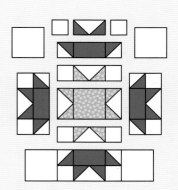

		FINISHED BLOCK SIZE					
		Single dimensions in the cutting chart indicate the size of the cut square (3" = 3" x 3").					
For 1 block:		6"	8"	9"	10"	12"	14"
Light	A: 2 ⊠→⊠	2¾"	3¼"	3½"	3¾"	4¼"	4¾"
	B: 4 ▢	2"	2½"	2¾"	3"	3½"	4"
	C: 4 ◺→◺	1⅝"	1⅞"	2"	2⅛"	2⅜"	2⅝"
	D: 12 ▢	1¼"	1½"	1⅝"	1¾"	2"	2¼"
Medium	E: 1 ▢	2"	2½"	2¾"	3"	3½"	4"
	F: 4 ◺→◺	1⅝"	1⅞"	2"	2⅛"	2⅜"	2⅝"
Dark	G: 4 ▭	1¼" x 2"	1½" x 2½"	1⅝" x 2¾"	1¾" x 3"	2" x 3½"	2¼" x 4"
	H: 8 ◺→◺	1⅝"	1⅞"	2"	2⅛"	2⅜"	2⅝"

Try this: Reverse the mediums and darks.

▢ Square(s)	◸→◺ Square(s) cut once diagonally to make half-square triangles	⊠→⊠ Square(s) cut twice diagonally to make quarter-square triangles	▭ Rectangle(s)

Cry of the Loon

3-Unit Grid

Color Illustration: page 17

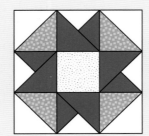 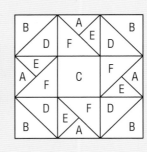 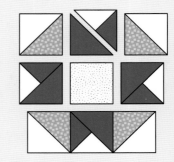

		FINISHED BLOCK SIZE					
			Single dimensions in the cutting chart indicate the size of the cut square (3" = 3" x 3").				
For 1 block:		4½"	6"	7½"	9"	10½"	12"
Light	A: 1	2¾"	3¼"	3¾"	4¼"	4¾"	5¼"
	B: 2	2⅜"	2⅞"	3⅜"	3⅞"	4⅜"	4⅞"
Light 2	C: 1	2"	2½"	3"	3½"	4"	4½"
Medium	D: 2	2⅜"	2⅞"	3⅜"	3⅞"	4⅜"	4⅞"
Dark	E: 1	2¾"	3¼"	3¾"	4¼"	4¾"	5¼"
	F: 2	2⅜"	2⅞"	3⅜"	3⅞"	4⅜"	4⅞"

Try this: Use one dark for E and a different dark for F.

Dewey Dream Quilt

5-Unit Grid

Color Illustration: page 17

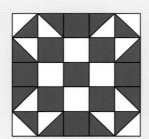 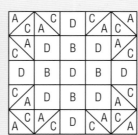 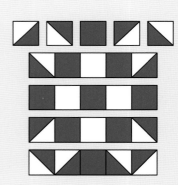

		FINISHED BLOCK SIZE					
			Single dimensions in the cutting chart indicate the size of the cut square (3" = 3" x 3").				
For 1 block:		5"	6¼"	7½"	8¾"	10"	12½"
Light	A: 6	1⅞"	2⅛"	2⅜"	2⅝"	2⅞"	3⅜"
	B: 4	1½"	1¾"	2"	2¼"	2½"	3"
Dark	C: 6	1⅞"	2⅛"	2⅜"	2⅝"	2⅞"	3⅜"
	D: 9	1½"	1¾"	2"	2¼"	2½"	3"

Try this: Use a medium instead of a dark for C.

Light   Light 2   Medium   Medium 2   Dark

Diagonal Square

4-Unit Grid

Color Illustration: page 17

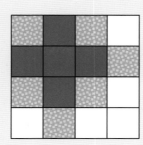

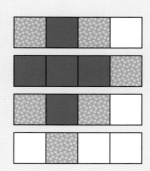

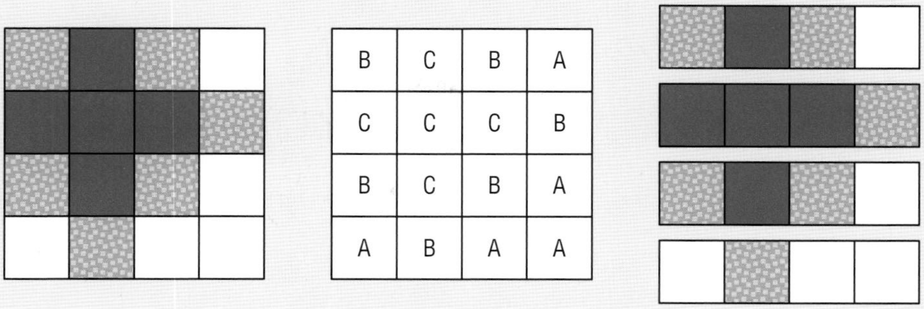

		FINISHED BLOCK SIZE				
		Single dimensions in the cutting chart indicate the size of the cut square (3" = 3" x 3").				
For 1 block:		4"	6"	8"	9"	10"	12"
Light	A: 5 ☐	1½"	2"	2½"	2¾"	3"	3½"
Medium	B: 6 ☐	1½"	2"	2½"	2¾"	3"	3½"
Dark	C: 5 ☐	1½"	2"	2½"	2¾"	3"	3½"

Try this: Use a different dark in every block.

Diamond Panes

7-Unit Grid

Color Illustration: page 17

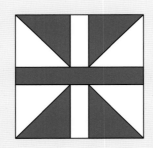

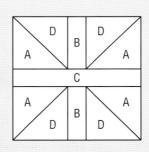

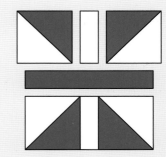

		FINISHED BLOCK SIZE				
		Single dimensions in the cutting chart indicate the size of the cut square (3" = 3" x 3").				
For 1 block:		5¼"	7"	8¾"	10½"	12¼"	14"
Light	A: 2 ◪→◩	3⅛"	3⅞"	4⅝"	5⅜"	6⅛"	6⅞"
	B: 2 ☐	1¼" x 2¾"	1½" x 3½"	1¾" x 4¼"	2" x 5"	2¼" x 5¾"	2½" x 6½"
Dark	C: 1 ☐	1¼" x 5¾"	1½" x 7½"	1¾" x 9¼"	2" x 11"	2¼" x 12¾"	2½" x 14½"
	D: 2 ◪→◩	3⅛"	3⅞"	4⅝"	5⅜"	6⅛"	6⅞"

Try this: Use one light for A and a different light for B.

☐ *Square(s)*   �diagonal *Square(s) cut once diagonally to make half-square triangles*   ⊠ *Square(s) cut twice diagonally to make quarter-square triangles*   ▭ *Rectangle(s)*

Diamond Plaid Block

9-Unit Grid

Color Illustration: page 17

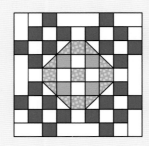

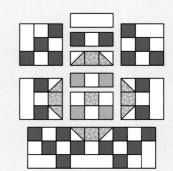

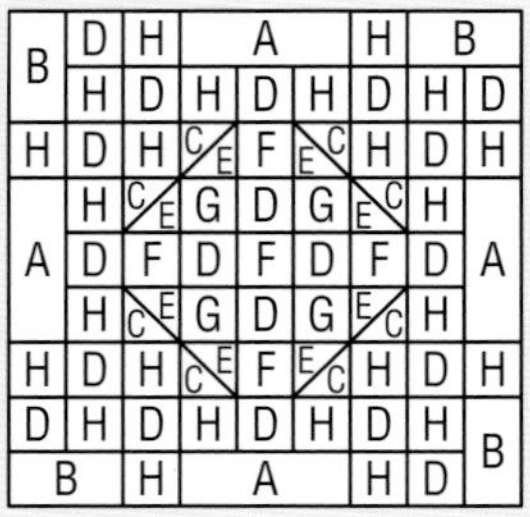

		FINISHED BLOCK SIZE					
		Single dimensions in the cutting chart indicate the size of the cut square (3" = 3" x 3").					
For 1 block:		6¾"	9"	10⅛"	11¼"	12⅜"	13½"
Light	A: 4	1¼" x 2¾"	1½" x 3½"	1⅝" x 3⅞"	1¾" x 4¼"	1⅞" x 4⅝"	2" x 5"
	B: 4	1¼" x 2"	1½" x 2½"	1⅝" x 2¾"	1¾" x 3"	1⅞" x 3¼"	2" x 3½"
	C: 4	1⅝"	1⅞"	2"	2⅛"	2¼"	2⅜"
	D: 20	1¼"	1½"	1⅝"	1¾"	1⅞"	2"
Medium	E: 4	1⅝"	1⅞"	2"	2⅛"	2¼"	2⅜"
	F: 5	1¼"	1½"	1⅝"	1¾"	1⅞"	2"
Medium 2	G: 4	1¼"	1½"	1⅝"	1¾"	1⅞"	2"
Dark	H: 24	1¼"	1½"	1⅝"	1¾"	1⅞"	2"

Try this: Use a different medium in every block.

Does Double Duty

5-Unit Grid

Color Illustration: page 17

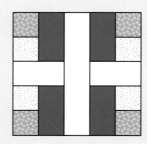
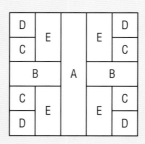
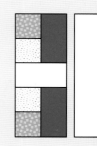
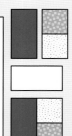

		FINISHED BLOCK SIZE					
		Single dimensions in the cutting chart indicate the size of the cut square (3" = 3" x 3").					
For 1 block:		5"	6¼"	7½"	8¾"	10"	12½"
Light	A: 1	1½" x 5½"	1¾" x 6¾"	2" x 8"	2¼" x 9¼"	2½" x 10½"	3" x 13"
	B: 2	1½" x 2½"	1¾" x 3"	2" x 3½"	2¼" x 4"	2½" x 4½"	3" x 5½"
Light 2	C: 4	1½"	1¾"	2"	2¼"	2½"	3"
Medium	D: 4	1½"	1¾"	2"	2¼"	2½"	3"
Dark	E: 4	1½" x 2½"	1¾" x 3"	2" x 3½"	2¼" x 4"	2½" x 4½"	3" x 5½"

Try this: Reverse the lights and darks in every other block.

☐ Light   ⬚ Light 2   ▨ Medium   ▨ Medium 2   ■ Dark

Domino Net

6-Unit Grid

Color Illustration: page 17

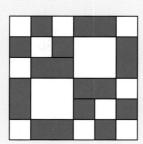

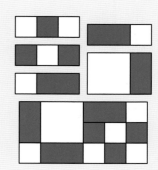

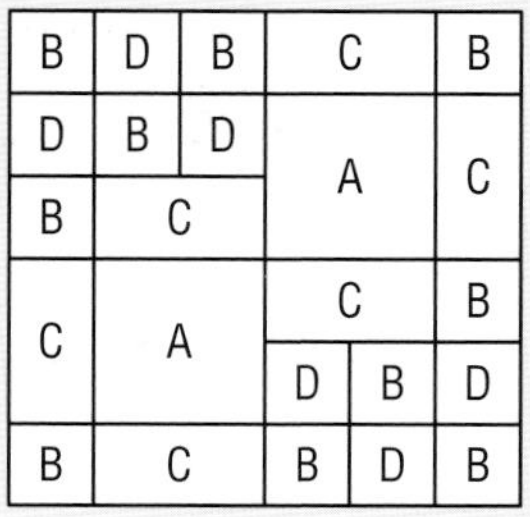

		FINISHED BLOCK SIZE					
		Single dimensions in the cutting chart indicate the size of the cut square (3" = 3" x 3").					
For 1 block:		4½"	6"	7½"	9"	10½"	12"
Light	A: 2 ☐	2"	2½"	3"	3½"	4"	4½"
	B: 10 ☐	1¼"	1½"	1¾"	2"	2¼"	2½"
Dark	C: 6 ▭	1¼" x 2"	1½" x 2½"	1¾" x 3"	2" x 3½"	2¼" x 4"	2½" x 4½"
	D: 6 ☐	1¼"	1½"	1¾"	2"	2¼"	2½"

Try this: Use a medium instead of a light for A.

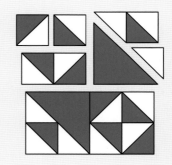

Double Cross II

4-Unit Grid

Color Illustration: page 17

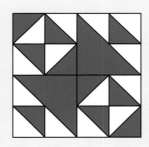

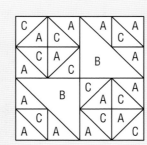

		FINISHED BLOCK SIZE					
		Single dimensions in the cutting chart indicate the size of the cut square (3" = 3" x 3").					
For 1 block:		4"	6"	8"	9"	10"	12"
Light	A: 7 ◩→◩	1⅞"	2⅜"	2⅞"	3⅛"	3⅜"	3⅞"
Dark	B: 1 ◩→◩	2⅞"	3⅞"	4⅞"	5⅜"	5⅞"	6⅞"
	C: 5 ◩→◩	1⅞"	2⅜"	2⅞"	3⅛"	3⅜"	3⅞"

Try this: Reverse the lights and darks.

☐ *Square(s)*   ◪→◩ *Square(s) cut once diagonally to make half-square triangles*   ⊠→⊠ *Square(s) cut twice diagonally to make quarter-square triangles*   ▭ *Rectangle(s)*

The Double V

5-Unit Grid

Color Illustration: page 17

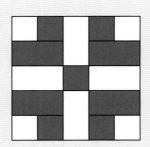

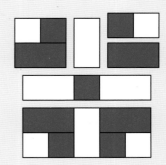

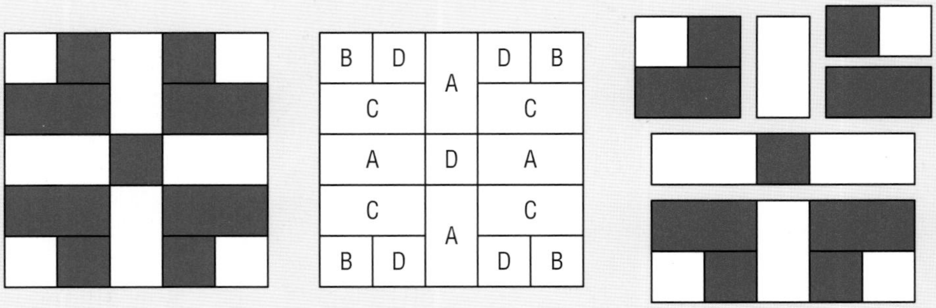

			FINISHED BLOCK SIZE					
			Single dimensions in the cutting chart indicate the size of the cut square (3" = 3" x 3").					
For 1 block:			5"	6¼"	7½"	8¾"	10"	12½"
Light	A: 4		1½" x 2½"	1¾" x 3"	2" x 3½"	2¼" x 4"	2½" x 4½"	3" x 5½"
	B: 4		1½"	1¾"	2"	2¼"	2½"	3"
Dark	C: 4		1½" x 2½"	1¾" x 3"	2" x 3½"	2¼" x 4"	2½" x 4½"	3" x 5½"
	D: 5		1½"	1¾"	2"	2¼"	2½"	3"

Try this: Use a medium instead of a light for A.

Duck's Foot

5-Unit Grid

Color Illustration: page 17

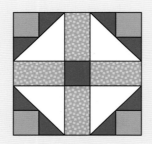

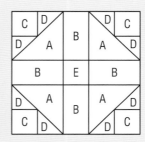

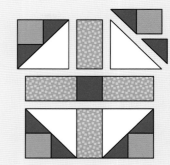

			FINISHED BLOCK SIZE					
			Single dimensions in the cutting chart indicate the size of the cut square (3" = 3" x 3").					
For 1 block:			5"	6¼"	7½"	8¾"	10"	12½"
Light	A: 2		2⅞"	3⅜"	3⅞"	4⅜"	4⅞"	5⅞"
Medium	B: 4		1½" x 2½"	1¾" x 3"	2" x 3½"	2¼" x 4"	2½" x 4½"	3" x 5½"
Medium 2	C: 4		1½"	1¾"	2"	2¼"	2½"	3"
Dark	D: 4		1⅞"	2⅛"	2⅜"	2⅝"	2⅞"	3⅜"
	E: 1		1½"	1¾"	2"	2¼"	2½"	3"

Try this: Use a light instead of medium 2 for C.

Light ⬜ Light 2 ▦ Medium ▨ Medium 2 ▨ Dark ■

Earthquake

4-Unit Grid

Color Illustration: page 18

Note: *This block is identical to Flying Geese II (page 68) in size, shape, and position of the pieces, but the value arrangement is different.*

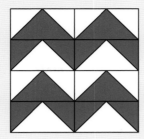
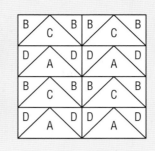
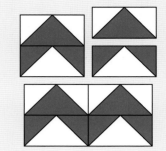

			FINISHED BLOCK SIZE					
			Single dimensions in the cutting chart indicate the size of the cut square (3" = 3" x 3").					
For 1 block:			4"	6"	8"	9"	10"	12"
Light	A: 1 ⊠→⊠		3¼"	4¼"	5¼"	5¾"	6¼"	7¼"
	B: 4 ◩→◹		1⅞"	2⅜"	2⅞"	3⅛"	3⅜"	3⅞"
Dark	C: 1 ⊠→⊠		3¼"	4¼"	5¼"	5¾"	6¼"	7¼"
	D: 4 ◩→◹		1⅞"	2⅜"	2⅞"	3⅛"	3⅜"	3⅞"

Try this: Use a medium instead of a light for A and B.

Eight Hands Around

8-Unit Grid

Color Illustration: page 18

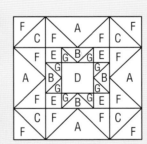

			FINISHED BLOCK SIZE					
			Single dimensions in the cutting chart indicate the size of the cut square (3" = 3" x 3").					
For 1 block:			6"	8"	9"	10"	12"	14"
Light	A: 1 ⊠→⊠		4¼"	5¼"	5¾"	6¼"	7¼"	8¼"
	B: 1 ⊠→⊠		2¾"	3¼"	3½"	3¾"	4¼"	4¾"
	C: 2 ◩→◹		2⅜"	2⅞"	3⅛"	3⅜"	3⅞"	4⅜"
	D: 1 ▢		2"	2½"	2¾"	3"	3½"	4"
	E: 4 ▢		1¼"	1½"	1⅝"	1¾"	2"	2¼"
Dark	F: 6 ◩→◹		2⅜"	2⅞"	3⅛"	3⅜"	3⅞"	4⅜"
	G: 4 ◩→◹		1⅝"	1⅞"	2"	2⅛"	2⅜"	2⅝"

Try this: Use one dark for F and a different dark for G.

▢ Square(s)	◩→◹ Square(s) cut once diagonally to make half-square triangles	⊠→⊠ Square(s) cut twice diagonally to make quarter-square triangles	▭ Rectangle(s)

An Envelope Motif

4-Unit Grid

Color Illustration: page 18

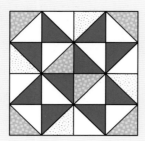
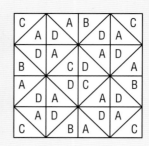
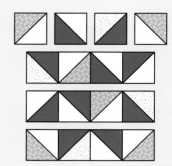

For 1 block:		FINISHED BLOCK SIZE					
		Single dimensions in the cutting chart indicate the size of the cut square (3" = 3" x 3").					
		4"	6"	8"	9"	10"	12"
Light	A: 6	1⅞"	2⅜"	2⅞"	3⅛"	3⅜"	3⅞"
Light 2	B: 2	1⅞"	2⅜"	2⅞"	3⅛"	3⅜"	3⅞"
Medium	C: 3	1⅞"	2⅜"	2⅞"	3⅛"	3⅜"	3⅞"
Dark	D: 5	1⅞"	2⅜"	2⅞"	3⅛"	3⅜"	3⅞"

Try this: Use a scrappy assortment of fabrics for A, B, and C.

Equinox

8-Unit Grid

Color Illustration: page 18

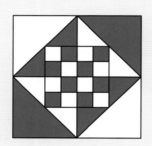
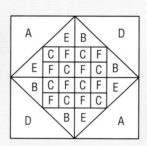
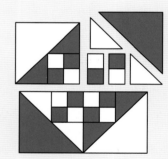

For 1 block:		FINISHED BLOCK SIZE					
		Single dimensions in the cutting chart indicate the size of the cut square (3" = 3" x 3").					
		6"	8"	9"	10"	12"	14"
Light	A: 1	3⅞"	4⅞"	5⅜"	5⅞"	6⅞"	7⅞"
	B: 2	2⅜"	2⅞"	3⅛"	3⅜"	3⅞"	4⅜"
	C: 8	1¼"	1½"	1⅝"	1¾"	2"	2¼"
Dark	D: 1	3⅞"	4⅞"	5⅜"	5⅞"	6⅞"	7⅞"
	E: 2	2⅜"	2⅞"	3⅛"	3⅜"	3⅞"	4⅜"
	F: 8	1¼"	1½"	1⅝"	1¾"	2"	2¼"

Try this: Use a different combination of lights and darks in each quadrant of the block.

☐ Light ☐ Light 2 ▨ Medium ▨ Medium 2 ■ Dark

Farm Friendliness

6-Unit Grid

Color Illustration: page 18

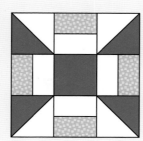 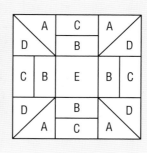 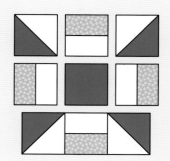

FINISHED BLOCK SIZE

Single dimensions in the cutting chart indicate the size of the cut square (3" = 3" x 3").

For 1 block:		4½"	6"	7½"	9"	10½"	12"
Light	A: 2 ▧→◩	2⅜"	2⅞"	3⅜"	3⅞"	4⅜"	4⅞"
	B: 4 ▭	1¼" x 2"	1½" x 2½"	1¾" x 3"	2" x 3½"	2¼" x 4"	2½" x 4½"
Medium	C: 4 ▭	1¼" x 2"	1½" x 2½"	1¾" x 3"	2" x 3½"	2¼" x 4"	2½" x 4½"
Dark	D: 2 ▧→◩	2⅜"	2⅞"	3⅜"	3⅞"	4⅜"	4⅞"
	E: 1 ▢	2"	2½"	3"	3½"	4"	4½"

Try this: Use one light for A and a different light for B.

Father's Choice

5-Unit Grid

Color Illustration: page 18

Note: *This block is identical to Five Patch Star (page 65) in size, shape, and position of the pieces, but the value arrangement is different.*

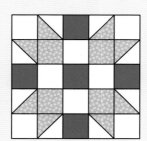 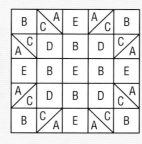 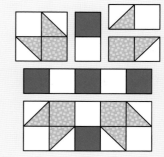

FINISHED BLOCK SIZE

Single dimensions in the cutting chart indicate the size of the cut square (3" = 3" x 3").

For 1 block:		5"	6¼"	7½"	8¾"	10"	12½"
Light	A: 4 ▧→◩	1⅞"	2⅛"	2⅜"	2⅝"	2⅞"	3⅜"
	B: 8 ▢	1½"	1¾"	2"	2¼"	2½"	3"
Medium	C: 4 ▧→◩	1⅞"	2⅛"	2⅜"	2⅝"	2⅞"	3⅜"
	D: 4 ▢	1½"	1¾"	2"	2¼"	2½"	3"
Dark	E: 5 ▢	1½"	1¾"	2"	2¼"	2½"	3"

Try this: Reverse the mediums and darks.

□ Square(s) ◰→◩ Square(s) cut once diagonally to make half-square triangles ⊠→⊠ Square(s) cut twice diagonally to make quarter-square triangles ▭ Rectangle(s)

Fields and Fences

11-Unit Grid

Color Illustration: page 18

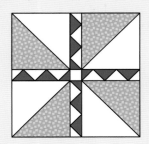
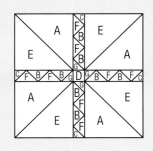
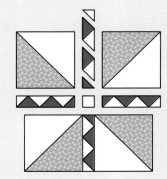

		FINISHED BLOCK SIZE					
		Single dimensions in the cutting chart indicate the size of the cut square (3" = 3" x 3").					
For 1 block:		6⅞"	8¼"	9⅝"	11"	12⅜"	15⅛"
Light	A: 2	4"	4⅝"	5¼"	5⅞"	6½"	7¾"
	B: 2	2½"	2¾"	3"	3¼"	3½"	4"
	C: 2	1½"	1⅝"	1¾"	1⅞"	2"	2¼"
	D: 1	1⅛"	1¼"	1⅜"	1½"	1⅝"	1⅞"
Medium	E: 2	4"	4⅝"	5¼"	5⅞"	6½"	7¾"
Dark	F: 2	2½"	2¾"	3"	3¼"	3½"	4"
	G: 2	1½"	1⅝"	1¾"	1⅞"	2"	2¼"

Try this: Use a different medium in every block.

Fireflies

4-Unit Grid

Color Illustration: page 18

Note: *This block is identical to Goose and Goslings (page 72) in size, shape, and position of the pieces, but the value arrangement is different.*

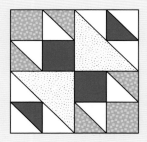
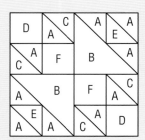
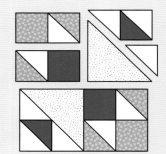

		FINISHED BLOCK SIZE					
		Single dimensions in the cutting chart indicate the size of the cut square (3" = 3" x 3").					
For 1 block:		4"	6"	8"	9"	10"	12"
Light	A: 5	1⅞"	2⅜"	2⅞"	3⅛"	3⅜"	3⅞"
Light 2	B: 1	2⅞"	3⅞"	4⅞"	5⅜"	5⅞"	6⅞"
Medium	C: 2	1⅞"	2⅜"	2⅞"	3⅛"	3⅜"	3⅞"
	D: 2	1½"	2"	2½"	2¾"	3"	3½"
Dark	E: 1	1⅞"	2⅜"	2⅞"	3⅛"	3⅜"	3⅞"
	F: 2	1½"	2"	2½"	2¾"	3"	3½"

Try this: Use a different combination of fabrics in every block.

☐ Light	▦ Light 2	▨ Medium ▨ Medium 2 ■ Dark

Five Patch Star

5-Unit Grid

Color Illustration: page 18

Note: *This block is identical to Father's Choice (page 63) in size, shape, and position of the pieces, but the value arrangement is different.*

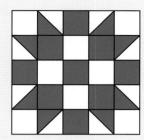

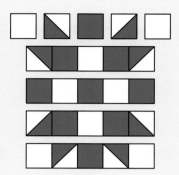

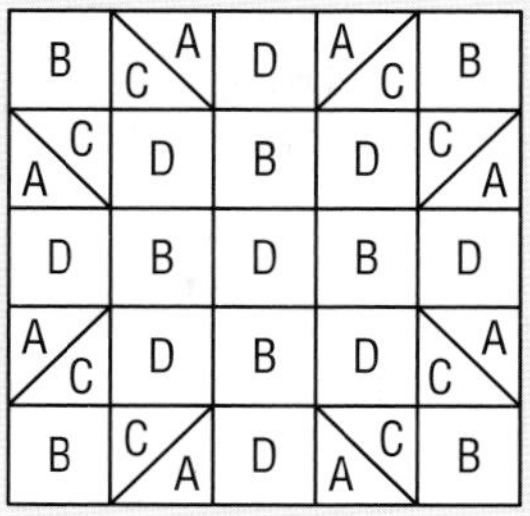

		FINISHED BLOCK SIZE					
		Single dimensions in the cutting chart indicate the size of the cut square (3" = 3" x 3").					
For 1 block:		5"	6¼"	7½"	8¾"	10"	12½"
Light	A: 4	1⅞"	2⅛"	2⅜"	2⅝"	2⅞"	3⅜"
	B: 8	1½"	1¾"	2"	2¼"	2½"	3"
Dark	C: 4	1⅞"	2⅛"	2⅜"	2⅝"	2⅞"	3⅜"
	D: 9	1½"	1¾"	2"	2¼"	2½"	3"

Try this: Reverse the lights and darks in every other block.

Flock of Birds

6-Unit Grid

Color Illustration: page 18

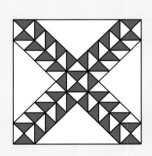

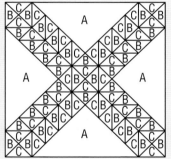

		FINISHED BLOCK SIZE					
		Single dimensions in the cutting chart indicate the size of the cut square (3" = 3" x 3").					
For 1 block:		4½"	6"	7½"	9"	10½"	12"
Light	A: 1	4¼"	5¼"	6¼"	7¼"	8¼"	9¼"
	B: 10	2"	2¼"	2½"	2¾"	3"	3¼"
Dark	C: 10	2"	2¼"	2½"	2¾"	3"	3¼"

Try this: Use many different darks for C.

 Square(s)   Square(s) cut once diagonally to make half-square triangles Square(s) cut twice diagonally to make quarter-square triangles   Rectangle(s)

Flower Basket

4-Unit Grid

Color Illustration: page 18

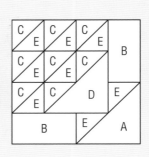
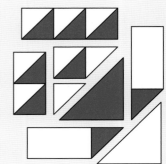

FINISHED BLOCK SIZE
Single dimensions in the cutting chart indicate the size of the cut square (3" = 3" x 3").

For 2 blocks:		4"	6"	8"	9"	10"	12"
Light	A: 1 ◻→◹	2⅞"	3⅞"	4⅞"	5⅜"	5⅞"	6⅞"
	B: 4 ▭	1½" x 2½"	2" x 3½"	2½" x 4½"	2¾" x 5"	3" x 5½"	3½" x 6½"
	C: 8 ◻→◹	1⅞"	2⅜"	2⅞"	3⅛"	3⅜"	3⅞"
Dark	D: 1 ◻→◹	2⅞"	3⅞"	4⅞"	5⅜"	5⅞"	6⅞"
	E: 8 ◻→◹	1⅞"	2⅜"	2⅞"	3⅛"	3⅜"	3⅞"

Try this: Use a medium instead of a dark for D and E.

Flower Pot II

4-Unit Grid

Color Illustration: page 18

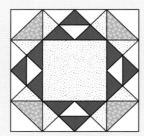
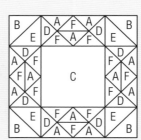

FINISHED BLOCK SIZE
Single dimensions in the cutting chart indicate the size of the cut square (3" = 3" x 3").

For 1 block:		4"	6"	8"	9"	10"	12"
Light	A: 3 ⊠→⊠	2¼"	2¾"	3¼"	3½"	3¾"	4¼"
	B: 2 ◻→◹	1⅞"	2⅜"	2⅞"	3⅛"	3⅜"	3⅞"
Light 2	C: 1 ◻	2½"	3½"	4½"	5"	5½"	6½"
	D: 2 ⊠→⊠	2¼"	2¾"	3¼"	3½"	3¾"	4¼"
Medium	E: 2 ◻→◹	1⅞"	2⅜"	2⅞"	3⅛"	3⅜"	3⅞"
Dark	F: 3 ⊠→⊠	2¼"	2¾"	3¼"	3½"	3¾"	4¼"

Try this: Use a different dark in every block.

◻ Light   ▨ Light 2   ▧ Medium   ▩ Medium 2   ■ Dark

Flyfoot

4-Unit Grid

Color Illustration: page 19

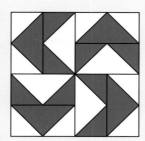 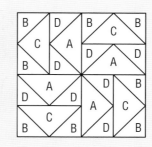 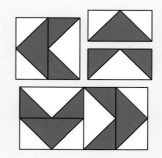

		FINISHED BLOCK SIZE					
		Single dimensions in the cutting chart indicate the size of the cut square (3" = 3" x 3").					
For 1 block:		4"	6"	8"	9"	10"	12"
Light	A: 1 ⊠→⊠	3¼"	4¼"	5¼"	5¾"	6¼"	7¼"
	B: 4 ◺→◺	1⅞"	2⅜"	2⅞"	3⅛"	3⅜"	3⅞"
Dark	C: 1 ⊠→⊠	3¼"	4¼"	5¼"	5¾"	6¼"	7¼"
	D: 4 ◺→◺	1⅞"	2⅜"	2⅞"	3⅛"	3⅜"	3⅞"

Try this: Use a different combination of fabrics in every block.

Flying Cloud

4-Unit Grid

Color Illustration: page 19

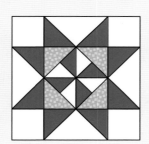 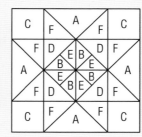 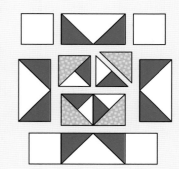

		FINISHED BLOCK SIZE					
		Single dimensions in the cutting chart indicate the size of the cut square (3" = 3" x 3").					
For 1 block:		4"	6"	8"	9"	10"	12"
Light	A: 1 ⊠→⊠	3¼"	4¼"	5¼"	5¾"	6¼"	7¼"
	B: 1 ⊠→⊠	2¼"	2¾"	3¼"	3½"	3¾"	4¼"
	C: 4 ☐	1½"	2"	2½"	2¾"	3"	3½"
Medium	D: 2 ◺→◺	1⅞"	2⅜"	2⅞"	3⅛"	3⅜"	3⅞"
Dark	E: 1 ⊠→⊠	2¼"	2¾"	3¼"	3½"	3¾"	4¼"
	F: 4 ◺→◺	1⅞"	2⅜"	2⅞"	3⅛"	3⅜"	3⅞"

Try this: Reverse the lights and mediums in every other block.

 Square(s)   Square(s) cut once diagonally to make half-square triangles   Square(s) cut twice diagonally to make quarter-square triangles   Rectangle(s)

Flying Geese II

4-Unit Grid

Color Illustration: page 19

Note: *This block is identical to Earthquake (page 61) in size, shape, and position of the pieces, but the value arrangement is different.*

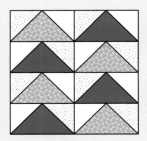 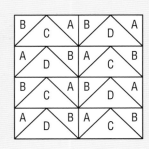 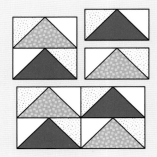

FINISHED BLOCK SIZE
Single dimensions in the cutting chart indicate the size of the cut square (3" = 3" x 3").

For 1 block:			4"	6"	8"	9"	10"	12"
Light	A: 4		1⅞"	2⅜"	2⅞"	3⅛"	3⅜"	3⅞"
Light 2	B: 4		1⅞"	2⅜"	2⅞"	3⅛"	3⅜"	3⅞"
Medium	C: 1		3¼"	4¼"	5¼"	5¾"	6¼"	7¼"
Dark	D: 1		3¼"	4¼"	5¼"	5¾"	6¼"	7¼"

Try this: Use a scrappy assortment of lights for A and B.

Foggy Mountain Breakdown

8-Unit Grid

Color Illustration: page 19

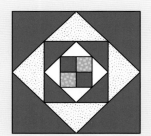 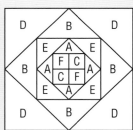 

FINISHED BLOCK SIZE
Single dimensions in the cutting chart indicate the size of the cut square (3" = 3" x 3").

For 1 block:			6"	8"	9"	10"	12"	14"
Light	A: 1		2¾"	3¼"	3½"	3¾"	4¼"	4¾"
Light 2	B: 1		4¼"	5¼"	5¾"	6¼"	7¼"	8¼"
Medium	C: 2		1¼"	1½"	1⅝"	1¾"	2"	2¼"
Dark	D: 2		3⅞"	4⅞"	5⅜"	5⅞"	6⅞"	7⅞"
	E: 2		2⅜"	2⅞"	3⅛"	3⅜"	3⅞"	4⅜"
	F: 2		1¼"	1½"	1⅝"	1¾"	2"	2¼"

Try this: Use a different combination of lights in every block.

Light   Light 2   Medium   Medium 2   Dark

Foot Stool

5-Unit Grid

Color Illustration: page 19

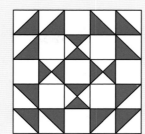 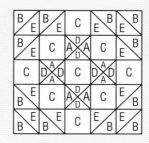 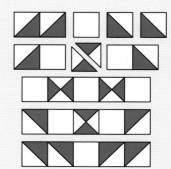

For 1 block:		FINISHED BLOCK SIZE					
		Single dimensions in the cutting chart indicate the size of the cut square (3" = 3" x 3").					
		5"	6¼"	7½"	8¾"	10"	12½"
Light	A: 2 ⊠→⊠	2¼"	2½"	2¾"	3"	3¼"	3¾"
	B: 6 ◹→◺	1⅞"	2⅛"	2⅜"	2⅝"	2⅞"	3⅜"
	C: 9 ◻	1½"	1¾"	2"	2¼"	2½"	3"
Dark	D: 2 ⊠→⊠	2¼"	2½"	2¾"	3"	3¼"	3¾"
	E: 6 ◹→◺	1⅞"	2⅛"	2⅜"	2⅝"	2⅞"	3⅜"

Try this: Use a medium instead of a dark for D.

Forest Paths

6-Unit Grid

Color Illustration: page 19

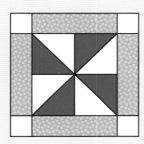 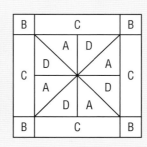 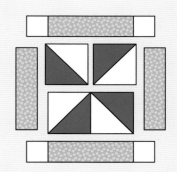

For 1 block:		FINISHED BLOCK SIZE					
		Single dimensions in the cutting chart indicate the size of the cut square (3" = 3" x 3").					
		4½"	6"	7½"	9"	10½"	12"
Light	A: 2 ◹→◺	2⅜"	2⅞"	3⅜"	3⅞"	4⅜"	4⅞"
	B: 4 ◻	1¼"	1½"	1¾"	2"	2¼"	2½"
Medium	C: 4 ▭	1¼" x 3½"	1½" x 4½"	1¾" x 5½"	2" x 6½"	2¼" x 7½"	2½" x 8½"
Dark	D: 2 ◹→◺	2⅜"	2⅞"	3⅜"	3⅞"	4⅜"	4⅞"

Try this: Reverse the lights and mediums in every other block.

| ◻ Square(s) | ◹→◺ Square(s) cut once diagonally to make half-square triangles | ⊠→⊠ Square(s) cut twice diagonally to make quarter-square triangles | ▭ Rectangle(s) |

Forget-Me-Nots

4-Unit Grid

Color Illustration: page 19

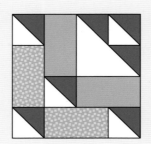 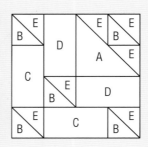 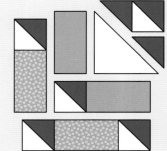

		FINISHED BLOCK SIZE					
		Single dimensions in the cutting chart indicate the size of the cut square (3" = 3" x 3").					
For 2 blocks:		4"	6"	8"	9"	10"	12"
Light	A: 1	2⅞"	3⅞"	4⅞"	5⅜"	5⅞"	6⅞"
	B: 5	1⅞"	2⅜"	2⅞"	3⅛"	3⅜"	3⅞"
Medium	C: 4	1½" x 2½"	2" x 3½"	2½" x 4½"	2¾" x 5"	3" x 5½"	3½" x 6½"
Medium 2	D: 4	1½" x 2½"	2" x 3½"	2½" x 4½"	2¾" x 5"	3" x 5½"	3½" x 6½"
Dark	E: 7	1⅞"	2⅜"	2⅞"	3⅛"	3⅜"	3⅞"

Try this: Use a different combination of lights and mediums in every block.

Foxy Grandpa

6-Unit Grid

Color Illustration: page 19

 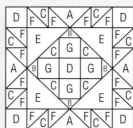 

		FINISHED BLOCK SIZE					
		Single dimensions in the cutting chart indicate the size of the cut square (3" = 3" x 3").					
For 1 block:		4½"	6"	7½"	9"	10½"	12"
Light	A: 1	2¾"	3¼"	3¾"	4¼"	4¾"	5¼"
	B: 1	2"	2¼"	2½"	2¾"	3"	3¼"
	C: 6	1⅝"	1⅞"	2⅛"	2⅜"	2⅝"	2⅞"
	D: 5	1¼"	1½"	1¾"	2"	2¼"	2½"
Dark	E: 2	2⅜"	2⅞"	3⅜"	3⅞"	4⅜"	4⅞"
	F: 8	1⅝"	1⅞"	2⅛"	2⅜"	2⅝"	2⅞"
	G: 4	1¼"	1½"	1¾"	2"	2¼"	2½"

Try this: Use a medium instead of a dark for G.

Gaggle of Geese

6-Unit Grid

Color Illustration: page 19

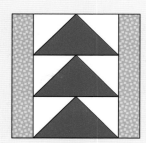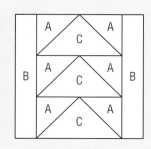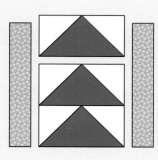

FINISHED BLOCK SIZE						
Single dimensions in the cutting chart indicate the size of the cut square (3" = 3" x 3").						
For 4 blocks:		4½"	6"	7½"	9"	10½"	12"
Light	A: 12 ◻▸◺	2⅜"	2⅞"	3⅜"	3⅞"	4⅜"	4⅞"
Medium	B: 8 ▭	1¼" x 5"	1½" x 6½"	1¾" x 8"	2" x 9½"	2¼" x 11"	2½" x 12½"
Dark	C: 3 ⊠▸⧅	4¼"	5¼"	6¼"	7¼"	8¼"	9¼"

Try this: Use several different darks for C.

Glorified Nine Patch

9-Unit Grid

Color Illustration: page 19

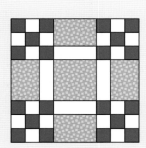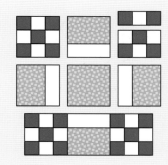

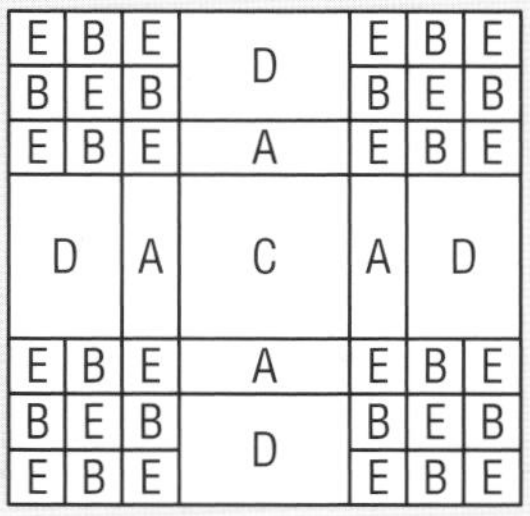

FINISHED BLOCK SIZE						
Single dimensions in the cutting chart indicate the size of the cut square (3" = 3" x 3").						
For 1 block:		6¾"	9"	10⅛"	11¼"	12⅜"	13½"
Light:	A: 4 ▭	1¼" x 2¾"	1½" x 3½"	1⅝" x 3⅞"	1¾" x 4¼"	1⅞" x 4⅝"	2" x 5"
	B: 16 ◻	1¼"	1½"	1⅝"	1¾"	1⅞"	2"
Medium	C: 1 ◻	2¾"	3½"	3⅞"	4¼"	4⅝"	5"
	D: 4 ▭	2" x 2¾"	2½" x 3½"	2¾" x 3⅞"	3" x 4¼"	3¼" x 4⅝"	3½" x 5"
Dark	E: 20 ◻	1¼"	1½"	1⅝"	1¾"	1⅞"	2"

Try this: Reverse the lights and mediums.

◻ *Square(s)*	◹▸◺ *Square(s) cut once diagonally to make half-square triangles*	⊠▸⧅ *Square(s) cut twice diagonally to make quarter-square triangles*	▭ *Rectangle(s)*

Golden Samovar

6-Unit Grid

Color Illustration: page 19

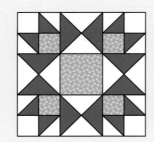
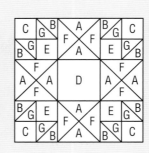
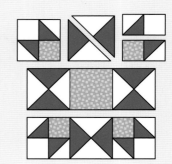

FINISHED BLOCK SIZE

Single dimensions in the cutting chart indicate the size of the cut square (3" = 3" x 3").

For 1 block:			4½"	6"	7½"	9"	10½"	12"
Light	A: 2		2¾"	3¼"	3¾"	4¼"	4¾"	5¼"
	B: 4		1⅝"	1⅞"	2⅛"	2⅜"	2⅝"	2⅞"
	C: 4		1¼"	1½"	1¾"	2"	2¼"	2½"
Medium	D: 1		2"	2½"	3"	3½"	4"	4½"
	E: 4		1¼"	1½"	1¾"	2"	2¼"	2½"
Dark	F: 2		2¾"	3¼"	3¾"	4¼"	4¾"	5¼"
	G: 4		1⅝"	1⅞"	2⅛"	2⅜"	2⅝"	2⅞"

Try this: Use one dark for F and a different dark for G.

Goose and Goslings

4-Unit Grid

Color Illustration: page 19

Note: *This block is identical to Fireflies (page 64) in size, shape, and position of the pieces, but the value arrangement is different.*

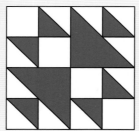
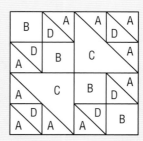
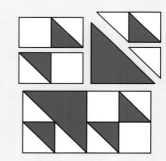

FINISHED BLOCK SIZE

Single dimensions in the cutting chart indicate the size of the cut square (3" = 3" x 3").

For 1 block:			4"	6"	8"	9"	10"	12"
Light	A: 5		1⅞"	2⅜"	2⅞"	3⅛"	3⅜"	3⅞"
	B: 4		1½"	2"	2½"	2¾"	3"	3½"
Dark	C: 1		2⅞"	3⅞"	4⅞"	5⅜"	5⅞"	6⅞"
	D: 3		1⅞"	2⅜"	2⅞"	3⅛"	3⅜"	3⅞"

Try this: Reverse the lights and darks.

☐ Light   ⬚ Light 2   ▦ Medium   ▨ Medium 2   ■ Dark

72

Grandma's Favorite

5-Unit Grid

Color Illustration: page 20

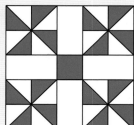
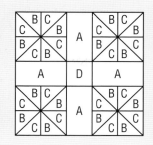
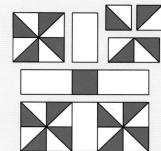

For 1 block:		FINISHED BLOCK SIZE					
		Single dimensions in the cutting chart indicate the size of the cut square (3" = 3" x 3").					
		5"	6¼"	7½"	8¾"	10"	12½"
Light	A: 4 ▭	1½" x 2½"	1¾" x 3"	2" x 3½"	2¼" x 4"	2½" x 4½"	3" x 5½"
	B: 8 ◻→◺	1⅞"	2⅛"	2⅜"	2⅝"	2⅞"	3⅜"
Dark	C: 8 ◻→◺	1⅞"	2⅛"	2⅜"	2⅝"	2⅞"	3⅜"
	D: 1 ◻	1½"	1¾"	2"	2¼"	2½"	3"

Try this: Use a medium instead of a light for A.

Grandma's Hop Scotch Quilt

3-Unit Grid

Color Illustration: page 20

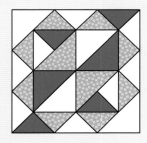
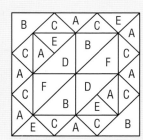

For 1 block:		FINISHED BLOCK SIZE					
		Single dimensions in the cutting chart indicate the size of the cut square (3" = 3" x 3").					
		4½"	6"	7½"	9"	10½"	12"
Light	A: 2 ⊠→⧅	2¾"	3¼"	3¾"	4¼"	4¾"	5¼"
	B: 2 ◻→◺	2⅜"	2⅞"	3⅜"	3⅞"	4⅜"	4⅞"
Medium	C: 2 ⊠→⧅	2¾"	3¼"	3¾"	4¼"	4¾"	5¼"
	D: 1 ◻→◺	2⅜"	2⅞"	3⅜"	3⅞"	4⅜"	4⅞"
Dark	E: 1 ⊠→⧅	2¾"	3¼"	3¾"	4¼"	4¾"	5¼"
	F: 1 ◻→◺	2⅜"	2⅞"	3⅜"	3⅞"	4⅜"	4⅞"

Try this: Use one medium for C and a different medium for D.

◻ Square(s)	◻→◺ Square(s) cut once diagonally to make half-square triangles	⊠→⧅ Square(s) cut twice diagonally to make quarter-square triangles	▭ Rectangle(s)

Grandmother's Choice II

5-Unit Grid

Color Illustration: page 20

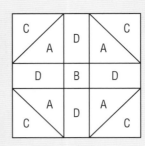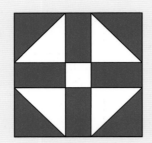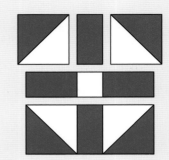

FINISHED BLOCK SIZE

Single dimensions in the cutting chart indicate the size of the cut square (3" = 3" x 3").

For 1 block:			5"	6¼"	7½"	8¾"	10"	12½"
Light	A: 2		2⅞"	3⅜"	3⅞"	4⅜"	4⅞"	5⅞"
	B: 1		1½"	1¾"	2"	2¼"	2½"	3"
Dark	C: 2		2⅞"	3⅜"	3⅞"	4⅜"	4⅞"	5⅞"
	D: 4		1½" x 2½"	1¾" x 3"	2" x 3½"	2¼" x 4"	2½" x 4½"	3" x 5½"

Try this: Use a different combination of lights and darks in every block.

Grandmother's Pinwheel

10-Unit Grid

Color Illustration: page 20

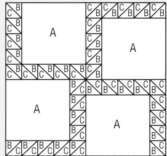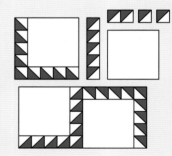

FINISHED BLOCK SIZE

Single dimensions in the cutting chart indicate the size of the cut square (3" = 3" x 3").

For 1 block:			6¼"	7½"	8¾"	10"	12½"	13¾"
Light	A: 4		3"	3½"	4"	4½"	5½"	6"
	B: 18		1½"	1⅝"	1¾"	1⅞"	2⅛"	2¼"
Dark	C: 18		1½"	1⅝"	1¾"	1⅞"	2⅛"	2¼"

Try this: Use many different darks for C.

☐ Light   ▨ Light 2   ▨ Medium   ▨ Medium 2   ■ Dark

Great Blue Heron

3-Unit Grid

Color Illustration: page 20

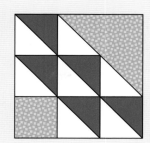
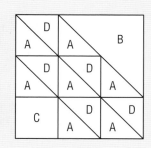
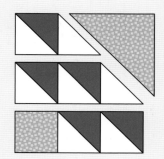

		FINISHED BLOCK SIZE				
		Single dimensions in the cutting chart indicate the size of the cut square (3" = 3" x 3").				
For 2 blocks:		4½"	6"	7½"	9"	10½"	12"
Light	A: 7 ◻→◺	2⅜"	2⅞"	3⅜"	3⅞"	4⅜"	4⅞"
Medium	B: 1 ◻→◺	3⅞"	4⅞"	5⅞"	6⅞"	7⅞"	8⅞"
	C: 2 ◻	2"	2½"	3"	3½"	4"	4½"
Dark	D: 5 ◻→◺	2⅜"	2⅞"	3⅜"	3⅞"	4⅜"	4⅞"

Try this: Use a different medium in every block.

Hanging Basket

12-Unit Grid

Color Illustration: page 20

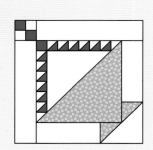
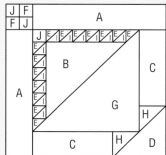
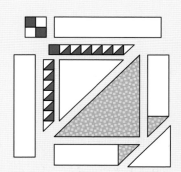

		FINISHED BLOCK SIZE				
		Single dimensions in the cutting chart indicate the size of the cut square (3" = 3" x 3").				
For 2 blocks:		6"	7½"	9"	12"	13½"	15"
Light	A: 4 ▭	1½" x 5½"	1¾" x 6¾"	2" x 8"	2½" x 10½"	2¾" x 11¾"	3" x 13"
	B: 1 ◻→◺	3⅞"	4⅝"	5⅜"	6⅞"	7⅝"	8⅜"
	C: 4 ▭	1½" x 3½"	1¾" x 4¼"	2" x 5"	2½" x 6½"	2¾" x 7¼ "	3" x 8"
	D: 1 ◻→◺	2⅞"	3⅜"	3⅞"	4⅞"	5⅜"	5⅞"
	E: 14 ◻→◺	1⅜"	1½"	1⅝"	1⅞"	2"	2⅛"
	F: 4 ◻	1"	1⅛"	1¼"	1½"	1⅝"	1¾"
Medium	G: 1 ◻→◺	4⅞"	5⅞"	6⅞"	8⅞"	9⅞"	10⅞"
	H: 2 ◻→◺	1⅞"	2⅛"	2⅜"	2⅞"	3⅛"	3⅜"
Dark	I: 12 ◻→◺	1⅜"	1½"	1⅝"	1⅞"	2"	2⅛"
	J: 6 ◻	1"	1⅛"	1¼"	1½"	1⅝"	1¾"

Try this: Use a different combination of fabrics in every block.

◻ Square(s)   ◻→◺ Square(s) cut once diagonally to make half-square triangles   ⊠→⊠ Square(s) cut twice diagonally to make quarter-square triangles   ▭ Rectangle(s)

Hayes Corner

6-Unit Grid

Color Illustration: page 20

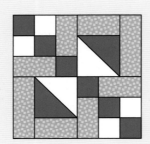
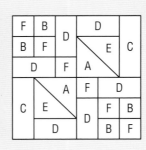
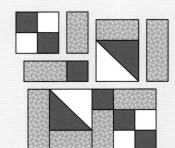

		FINISHED BLOCK SIZE					
		Single dimensions in the cutting chart indicate the size of the cut square (3" = 3" x 3").					
For 1 block:		4½"	6"	7½"	9"	10½"	12"
Light	A: 1	2⅜"	2⅞"	3⅜"	3⅞"	4⅜"	4⅞"
	B: 4	1¼"	1½"	1¾"	2"	2¼"	2½"
Medium	C: 2	1¼" x 2¾"	1½" x 3½"	1¾" x 4¼"	2" x 5"	2¼" x 5¾"	2½" x 6½"
	D: 6	1¼" x 2"	1½" x 2½"	1¾" x 3"	2" x 3½"	2¼" x 4"	2½" x 4½"
Dark	E: 1	2⅜"	2⅞"	3⅜"	3⅞"	4⅜"	4⅞"
	F: 6	1¼"	1½"	1¾"	2"	2¼"	2½"

Try this: Use a different medium in every block.

The Hen and Her Chicks

8-Unit Grid

Color Illustration: page 20

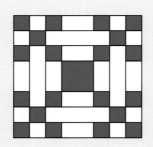

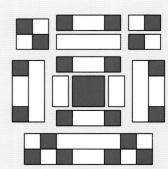

		FINISHED BLOCK SIZE					
		Single dimensions in the cutting chart indicate the size of the cut square (3" = 3" x 3").					
For 1 block:		6"	8"	9"	10"	12"	14"
Light	A: 4	1¼" x 3½"	1½" x 4½"	1⅝" x 5"	1¾" x 5½"	2" x 6½"	2¼" x 7½"
	B: 8	1¼" x 2"	1½" x 2½"	1⅝" x 2¾"	1¾" x 3"	2" x 3½"	2¼" x 4"
	C: 8	1¼"	1½"	1⅝"	1¾"	2"	2¼"
Dark	D: 1	2"	2½"	2¾"	3"	3½"	4"
	E: 20	1¼"	1½"	1⅝"	1¾"	2"	2¼"

Try this: Use a medium instead of a light for B.

Light   Light 2   Medium   Medium 2   Dark

Herm's Shirt

4-Unit Grid

Color Illustration: page 20

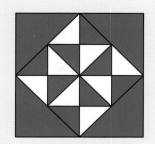
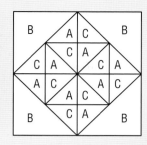

		FINISHED BLOCK SIZE					
		Single dimensions in the cutting chart indicate the size of the cut square (3" = 3" x 3").					
For 1 block:		4"	6"	8"	9"	10"	12"
Light	A: 4	1⅞"	2⅜"	2⅞"	3⅛"	3⅜"	3⅞"
Dark	B: 2	2⅞"	3⅞"	4⅞"	5⅜"	5⅞"	6⅞"
	C: 4	1⅞"	2⅜"	2⅞"	3⅛"	3⅜"	3⅞"

Try this: Reverse the lights and darks in every other block.

Hill and Valley

6-Unit Grid

Color Illustration: page 20

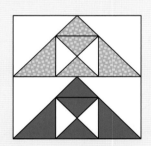
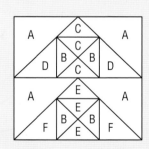

		FINISHED BLOCK SIZE					
		Single dimensions in the cutting chart indicate the size of the cut square (3" = 3" x 3").					
For 4 blocks:		4½"	6"	7½"	9"	10½"	12"
Light	A: 8	3⅛"	3⅞"	4⅝"	5⅜"	6⅛"	6⅞"
	B: 4	2¾"	3¼"	3¾"	4¼"	4¾"	5¼"
Medium	C: 3	2¾"	3¼"	3¾"	4¼"	4¾"	5¼"
	D: 4	2⅜"	2⅞"	3⅜"	3⅞"	4⅜"	4⅞"
Dark	E: 3	2¾"	3¼"	3¾"	4¼"	4¾"	5¼"
	F: 4	2⅜"	2⅞"	3⅜"	3⅞"	4⅜"	4⅞"

Try this: Use a different combination of mediums and darks in every block.

☐ *Square(s)*   ◺→◿ *Square(s) cut once diagonally to make half-square triangles*   ⊠→⧖ *Square(s) cut twice diagonally to make quarter-square triangles*   ▭ *Rectangle(s)*

Hollis Star

4-Unit Grid

Color Illustration: page 20

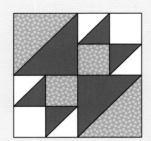
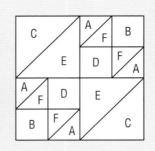
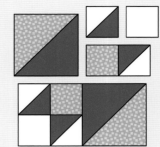

		FINISHED BLOCK SIZE					
		Single dimensions in the cutting chart indicate the size of the cut square (3" = 3" x 3").					
For 1 block:		4"	6"	8"	9"	10"	12"
Light	A: 2 ◻→◨	1⅞"	2⅜"	2⅞"	3⅛"	3⅜"	3⅞"
	B: 2 ◻	1½"	2"	2½"	2¾"	3"	3½"
Medium	C: 1 ◻→◨	2⅞"	3⅞"	4⅞"	5⅜"	5⅞"	6⅞"
	D: 2 ◻	1½"	2"	2½"	2¾"	3"	3½"
Dark	E: 1 ◻→◨	2⅞"	3⅞"	4⅞"	5⅜"	5⅞"	6⅞"
	F: 2 ◻→◨	1⅞"	2⅜"	2⅞"	3⅛"	3⅜"	3⅞"

Try this: Use one medium for C and a different medium for D.

Home Treasure

8-Unit Grid

Color Illustration: page 20

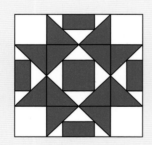
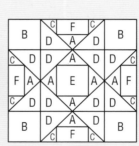

		FINISHED BLOCK SIZE					
		Single dimensions in the cutting chart indicate the size of the cut square (3" = 3" x 3").					
For 1 block:		6"	8"	9"	10"	12"	14"
Light	A: 2 ⊠→⊠	2¾"	3¼"	3½"	3¾"	4¼"	4¾"
	B: 4 ◻	2"	2½"	2¾"	3"	3½"	4"
	C: 4 ◻→◨	1⅝"	1⅞"	2"	2⅛"	2⅜"	2⅝"
Dark	D: 6 ◻→◨	2⅜"	2⅞"	3⅛"	3⅜"	3⅞"	4⅜"
	E: 1 ◻	2"	2½"	2¾"	3"	3½"	4"
	F: 4 ▭	1¼" x 2"	1½" x 2½"	1⅝" x 2¾"	1¾" x 3"	2" x 3½"	2¼" x 4"

Try this: Use a medium instead of a dark for E and F.

Homeward Bound

2-Unit Grid

Color Illustration: page 21

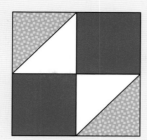 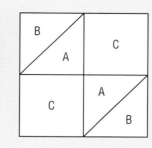 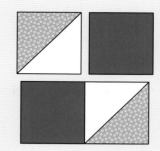

				FINISHED BLOCK SIZE			
				Single dimensions in the cutting chart indicate the size of the cut square (3" = 3" x 3").			
For 1 block:			4"	6"	8"	9"	10"	12"

For 1 block:		4"	6"	8"	9"	10"	12"
Light	A: 1	2⅞"	3⅞"	4⅞"	5⅜"	5⅞"	6⅞"
Medium	B: 1	2⅞"	3⅞"	4⅞"	5⅜"	5⅞"	6⅞"
Dark	C: 2	2½"	3½"	4½"	5"	5½"	6½"

Try this: Reverse the lights and mediums in every other block.

Hopkins Square

4-Unit Grid

Color Illustration: page 21

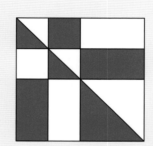 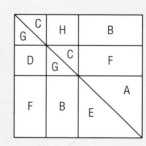 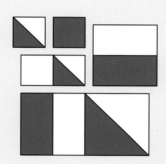

FINISHED BLOCK SIZE
Single dimensions in the cutting chart indicate the size of the cut square (3" = 3" x 3").

For 2 blocks:		4"	6"	8"	9"	10"	12"
Light	A: 1	2⅞"	3⅞"	4⅞"	5⅜"	5⅞"	6⅞"
	B: 4	1½" x 2½"	2" x 3½"	2½" x 4½"	2¾" x 5"	3" x 5½"	3½" x 6½"
	C: 2	1⅞"	2⅜"	2⅞"	3⅛"	3⅜"	3⅞"
	D: 2	1½"	2"	2½"	2¾"	3"	3½"
Dark	E: 1	2⅞"	3⅞"	4⅞"	5⅜"	5⅞"	6⅞"
	F: 4	1½" x 2½"	2" x 3½"	2½" x 4½"	2¾" x 5"	3" x 5½"	3½" x 6½"
	G: 2	1⅞"	2⅜"	2⅞"	3⅛"	3⅜"	3⅞"
	H: 2	1½"	2"	2½"	2¾"	3"	3½"

Try this: Use one light for A and C and a different light for B and D.

 Square(s)   *Square(s) cut once diagonally to make half-square triangles*   ☒ *Square(s) cut twice diagonally to make quarter-square triangles*   ☐ *Rectangle(s)*

Hour Glass #2

3-Unit Grid

Color Illustration: page 21

Note: *This block is identical to Practical Orchard II (page 99) in size, shape, and position of the pieces, but the value arrangement is different.*

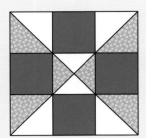

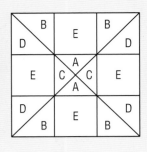

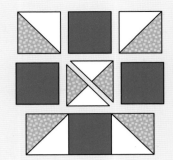

			FINISHED BLOCK SIZE				
			Single dimensions in the cutting chart indicate the size of the cut square (3" = 3" x 3").				
For 2 blocks:			4½"	6"	7½"	9"	10½"	12"
Light	A: 1 ⊠→⊠	2¾"	3¼"	3¾"	4¼"	4¾"	5¼"
	B: 4 ◻→◺	2⅜"	2⅞"	3⅜"	3⅞"	4⅜"	4⅞"
Medium	C: 1 ⊠→⊠	2¾"	3¼"	3¾"	4¼"	4¾"	5¼"
	D: 4 ◻→◺	2⅜"	2⅞"	3⅜"	3⅞"	4⅜"	4⅞"
Dark	E: 8 ◻	2"	2½"	3"	3½"	4"	4½"

Try this: Reverse the mediums and darks in every other block.

Hour Glass III

3-Unit Grid

Color Illustration: page 21

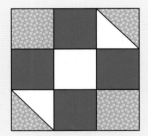

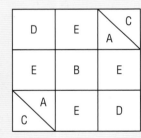

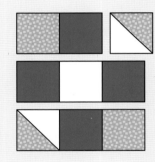

			FINISHED BLOCK SIZE				
			Single dimensions in the cutting chart indicate the size of the cut square (3" = 3" x 3").				
For 1 block:			4½"	6"	7½"	9"	10½"	12"
Light	A: 1 ◻→◺	2⅜"	2⅞"	3⅜"	3⅞"	4⅜"	4⅞"
	B: 1 ◻	2"	2½"	3"	3½"	4"	4½"
Medium	C: 1 ◻→◺	2⅜"	2⅞"	3⅜"	3⅞"	4⅜"	4⅞"
	D: 2 ◻	2"	2½"	3"	3½"	4"	4½"
Dark	E: 4 ◻	2"	2½"	3"	3½"	4"	4½"

Try this: Use a different combination of fabrics in every block.

◻ Light ⬚ Light 2 ▦ Medium ▨ Medium 2 ■ Dark

Hour Glass IV

6-Unit Grid

Color Illustration: page 21

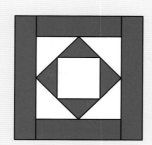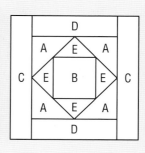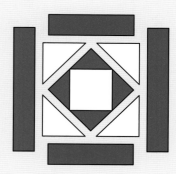

		FINISHED BLOCK SIZE					
		Single dimensions in the cutting chart indicate the size of the cut square (3" = 3" x 3").					
For 1 block:		4½"	6"	7½"	9"	10½"	12"
Light	A: 2	2⅜"	2⅞"	3⅜"	3⅞"	4⅜"	4⅞"
	B: 1	2"	2½"	3"	3½"	4"	4½"
Dark	C: 2	1¼" x 5"	1½" x 6½"	1¾" x 8"	2" x 9½"	2¼" x 11"	2½" x 12½"
	D: 2	1¼" x 3½"	1½" x 4½"	1¾" x 5½"	2" x 6½"	2¼" x 7½"	2½" x 8½"
	E: 1	2¾"	3¼"	3¾"	4¼"	4¾"	5¼"

Try this: Reverse the lights and darks in every other block.

Jack in the Box

5-Unit Grid

Color Illustration: page 21

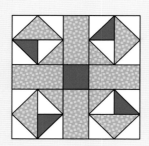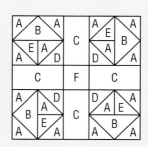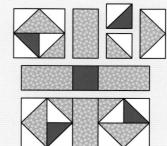

		FINISHED BLOCK SIZE					
		Single dimensions in the cutting chart indicate the size of the cut square (3" = 3" x 3").					
For 1 block:		5"	6¼"	7½"	8¾"	10"	12½"
Light	A: 8	1⅞"	2⅛"	2⅜"	2⅝"	2⅞"	3⅜"
Medium	B: 1	3¼"	3¾"	4¼"	4¾"	5¼"	6¼"
	C: 4	1½" x 2½"	1¾" x 3"	2" x 3½"	2¼" x 4"	2½" x 4½"	3" x 5½"
	D: 2	1⅞"	2⅛"	2⅜"	2⅝"	2⅞"	3⅜"
Dark	E: 2	1⅞"	2⅛"	2⅜"	2⅝"	2⅞"	3⅜"
	F: 1	1½"	1¾"	2"	2¼"	2½"	3"

Try this: Use one medium for C and a different medium for B and D.

81

Janet's Star

6-Unit Grid

Color Illustration: page 21

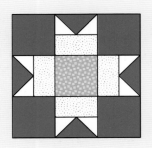
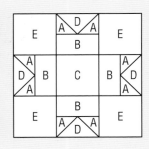
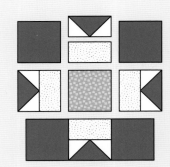

For 1 block:		FINISHED BLOCK SIZE					
		Single dimensions in the cutting chart indicate the size of the cut square (3" = 3" x 3").					
		4½"	6"	7½"	9"	10½"	12"
Light	A: 4	1⅝"	1⅞"	2⅛"	2⅜"	2⅝"	2⅞"
Light 2	B: 4 ▭	1¼" x 2"	1½" x 2½"	1¾" x 3"	2" x 3½"	2¼" x 4"	2½" x 4½"
Medium	C: 1 ▢	2"	2½"	3"	3½"	4"	4½"
Dark	D: 1 ⊠	2¾"	3¼"	3¾"	4¼"	4¾"	5¼"
	E: 4 ▢	2"	2½"	3"	3½"	4"	4½"

Try this: Use a different dark in every block.

Judy's Choice

5-Unit Grid

Color Illustration: page 21

Note: *This block is identical to Vice President's Block (page 124) in size, shape, and position of the pieces, but the value arrangement is different.*

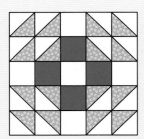
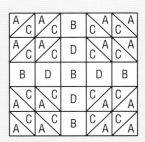
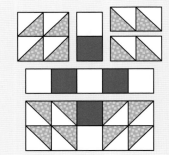

For 1 block:		FINISHED BLOCK SIZE					
		Single dimensions in the cutting chart indicate the size of the cut square (3" = 3" x 3").					
		5"	6¼"	7½"	8¾"	10"	12½"
Light	A: 8	1⅞"	2⅛"	2⅜"	2⅝"	2⅞"	3⅜"
	B: 5 ▢	1½"	1¾"	2"	2¼"	2½"	3"
Medium	C: 8	1⅞"	2⅛"	2⅜"	2⅝"	2⅞"	3⅜"
Dark	D: 4 ▢	1½"	1¾"	2"	2¼"	2½"	3"

Try this: Use several different mediums for C.

▢ Light   ▦ Light 2   ▨ Medium   ▩ Medium 2   ■ Dark

King's Crown II

5-Unit Grid

Color Illustration: page 21

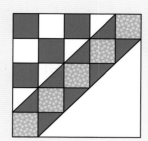 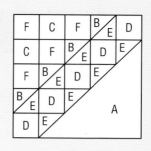 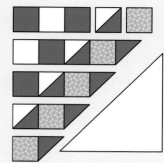

		FINISHED BLOCK SIZE					
		Single dimensions in the cutting chart indicate the size of the cut square (3" = 3" x 3").					
For 2 blocks:		5"	6¼"	7½"	8¾"	10"	12½"
Light	A: 1 ◻→◺	4⅞"	5⅞"	6⅞"	7⅞"	8⅞"	10⅞"
	B: 4 ◻→◺	1⅞"	2⅛"	2⅜"	2⅝"	2⅞"	3⅜"
	C: 4 ◻	1½"	1¾"	2"	2¼"	2½"	3"
Medium	D: 10 ◻	1½"	1¾"	2"	2¼"	2½"	3"
Dark	E: 8 ◻→◺	1⅞"	2⅛"	2⅜"	2⅝"	2⅞"	3⅜"
	F: 8 ◻	1½"	1¾"	2"	2¼"	2½"	3"

Try this: Use a large-scale print for A.

The Letter X

3-Unit Grid

Color Illustration: page 21

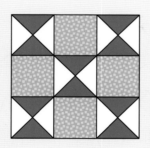 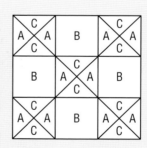 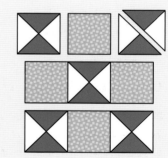

		FINISHED BLOCK SIZE					
		Single dimensions in the cutting chart indicate the size of the cut square (3" = 3" x 3").					
For 2 blocks:		4½"	6"	7½"	9"	10½"	12"
Light	A: 5 ⊠→⧇	2¾"	3¼"	3¾"	4¼"	4¾"	5¼"
Medium	B: 8 ◻	2"	2½"	3"	3½"	4"	4½"
Dark	C: 5 ⊠→⧇	2¾"	3¼"	3¾"	4¼"	4¾"	5¼"

Try this: Reverse the mediums and darks in every other block.

◻ Square(s) ◻→◺ Square(s) cut once diagonally to make half-square triangles ⊠→⧇ Square(s) cut twice diagonally to make quarter-square triangles ▭ Rectangle(s)

Light and Shadows

4-Unit Grid

Color Illustration: page 21

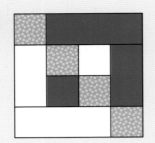
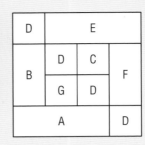
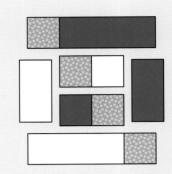

		FINISHED BLOCK SIZE Single dimensions in the cutting chart indicate the size of the cut square (3" = 3" x 3").					
For 1 block:		4"	6"	8"	9"	10"	12"
Light	A: 1	1½" x 3½"	2" x 5"	2½" x 6½"	2¾" x 7¼"	3" x 8"	3½" x 9½"
	B: 1	1½" x 2½"	2" x 3½"	2½" x 4½"	2¾" x 5"	3" x 5½"	3½" x 6½"
	C: 1	1½"	2"	2½"	2¾"	3"	3½"
Medium	D: 4	1½"	2"	2½"	2¾"	3"	3½"
Dark	E: 1	1½" x 3½"	2" x 5"	2½" x 6½"	2¾" x 7¼"	3" x 8"	3½" x 9½"
	F: 1	1½" x 2½"	2" x 3½"	2½" x 4½"	2¾" x 5"	3" x 5½"	3½" x 6½"
	G: 1	1½"	2"	2½"	2¾"	3"	3½"

Try this: Use a different combination of lights and darks in every block.

Light	Light 2	Medium	Medium 2	Dark

Lighthouse

10-Unit Grid

Color Illustration: page 21

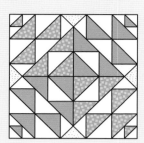
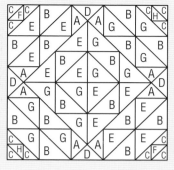

		FINISHED BLOCK SIZE					
		Single dimensions in the cutting chart indicate the size of the cut square (3" = 3" x 3").					
For 1 block:		6¼"	7½"	8¾"	10"	12½"	13¾"
Light	A: 2 ☒→☒	2½"	2¾"	3"	3¼"	3¾"	4"
	B: 8 ◻→◺	2⅛"	2⅜"	2⅝"	2⅞"	3⅜"	3⅝"
	C: 6 ◻→◺	1½"	1⅝"	1¾"	1⅞"	2⅛"	2¼"
Light 2	D: 1 ☒→☒	2½"	2¾"	3"	3¼"	3¾"	4"
Medium	E: 6 ◻→◺	2⅛"	2⅜"	2⅝"	2⅞"	3⅜"	3⅝"
	F: 1 ◻→◺	1½"	1⅝"	1¾"	1⅞"	2⅛"	2¼"
Medium 2	G: 6 ◻→◺	2⅛"	2⅜"	2⅝"	2⅞"	3⅜"	3⅝"
	H: 1 ◻→◺	1½"	1⅝"	1¾"	1⅞"	2⅛"	2¼"

Try this: Use a dark instead of medium 2 for G and H.

Lincoln's Platform

7-Unit Grid

Color Illustration: page 22

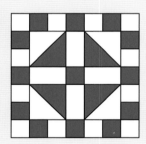
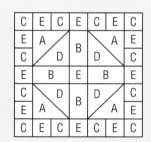
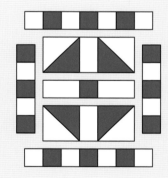

		FINISHED BLOCK SIZE					
		Single dimensions in the cutting chart indicate the size of the cut square (3" = 3" x 3").					
For 1 block:		5¼"	7"	8¾"	10½"	12¼"	14"
Light	A: 2 ◻→◺	2⅜"	2⅞"	3⅜"	3⅞"	4⅜"	4⅞"
	B: 4 ▭	1¼" x 2"	1½" x 2½"	1¾" x 3"	2" x 3½"	2¼" x 4"	2½" x 4½"
	C: 12 ◻	1¼"	1½"	1¾"	2"	2¼"	2½"
Dark	D: 2 ◻→◺	2⅜"	2⅞"	3⅜"	3⅞"	4⅜"	4⅞"
	E: 13 ◻	1¼"	1½"	1¾"	2"	2¼"	2½"

Try this: Use one dark for D and a different dark for E.

◻ Square(s)	◻→◺ Square(s) cut once diagonally to make half-square triangles	☒→☒ Square(s) cut twice diagonally to make quarter-square triangles	▭ Rectangle(s)

Lois' Star

11-Unit Grid

Color Illustration: page 22

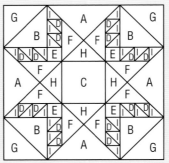

For 1 block:			FINISHED BLOCK SIZE					
			Single dimensions in the cutting chart indicate the size of the cut square (3" = 3" x 3").					
			6⅞"	8¼"	9⅝"	11"	12⅜"	15⅛"
Light	A: 1		4⅜"	5"	5⅝"	6¼"	6⅞"	8⅛"
	B: 2		2¾"	3⅛"	3½"	3⅞"	4¼"	5"
	C: 1		2⅜"	2¾"	3⅛"	3½"	3⅞"	4⅝"
	D: 8		1½"	1⅝"	1¾"	1⅞"	2"	2¼"
	E: 4		1⅛"	1¼"	1⅜"	1½"	1⅝"	1⅞"
Medium	F: 2		3⅛"	3½"	3⅞"	4¼"	4⅝"	5⅜"
	G: 2		2¾"	3⅛"	3½"	3⅞"	4¼"	5"
Dark	H: 1		3⅛"	3½"	3⅞"	4¼"	4⅝"	5⅜"
	I: 12		1½"	1⅝"	1¾"	1⅞"	2"	2¼"

Try this: Use a different medium in every block.

Light   Light 2   Medium   Medium 2   Dark

London Roads

9-Unit Grid

Color Illustration: page 22

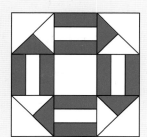
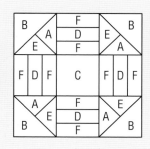
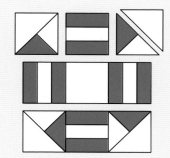

		FINISHED BLOCK SIZE					
		Single dimensions in the cutting chart indicate the size of the cut square (3" = 3" x 3").					
For 1 block:		6³⁄₄"	9"	10¹⁄₈"	11¹⁄₄"	12³⁄₈"	13¹⁄₂"
Light	A: 1	3¹⁄₂"	4¹⁄₄"	4⁵⁄₈"	5"	5³⁄₈"	5³⁄₄"
	B: 2	3¹⁄₈"	3⁷⁄₈"	4¹⁄₄"	4⁵⁄₈"	5"	5³⁄₈"
	C: 1	2³⁄₄"	3¹⁄₂"	3⁷⁄₈"	4¹⁄₄"	4⁵⁄₈"	5"
	D: 4	1¹⁄₄" x 2³⁄₄"	1¹⁄₂" x 3¹⁄₂"	1⁵⁄₈" x 3⁷⁄₈"	1³⁄₄" x 4¹⁄₄"	1⁷⁄₈" x 4⁵⁄₈"	2" x 5"
Dark	E: 1	3¹⁄₂"	4¹⁄₄"	4⁵⁄₈"	5"	5³⁄₈"	5³⁄₄"
	F: 8	1¹⁄₄" x 2³⁄₄"	1¹⁄₂" x 3¹⁄₂"	1⁵⁄₈" x 3⁷⁄₈"	1³⁄₄" x 4¹⁄₄"	1⁷⁄₈" x 4⁵⁄₈"	2" x 5"

Try this: Reverse the lights and darks in every other block.

Lover's Lane

6-Unit Grid

Color Illustration: page 22

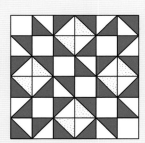
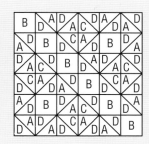
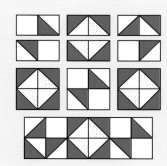

		FINISHED BLOCK SIZE					
		Single dimensions in the cutting chart indicate the size of the cut square (3" = 3" x 3").					
For 1 block:		4¹⁄₂"	6"	7¹⁄₂"	9"	10¹⁄₂"	12"
Light	A: 10	1⁵⁄₈"	1⁷⁄₈"	2¹⁄₈"	2³⁄₈"	2⁵⁄₈"	2⁷⁄₈"
	B: 8	1¹⁄₄"	1¹⁄₂"	1³⁄₄"	2"	2¹⁄₄"	2¹⁄₂"
Light 2	C: 4	1⁵⁄₈"	1⁷⁄₈"	2¹⁄₈"	2³⁄₈"	2⁵⁄₈"	2⁷⁄₈"
Dark	D: 14	1⁵⁄₈"	1⁷⁄₈"	2¹⁄₈"	2³⁄₈"	2⁵⁄₈"	2⁷⁄₈"

Try this: Use a medium instead of a light for B.

☐ Square(s)   ◻→◺ Square(s) cut once diagonally to make half-square triangles   ⊠→◳ Square(s) cut twice diagonally to make quarter-square triangles   ▭ Rectangle(s)

Maryland Beauty

10-Unit Grid

Color Illustration: page 22

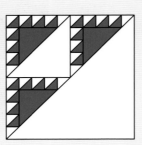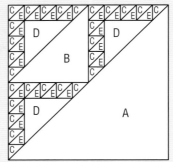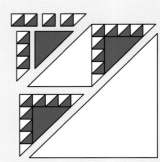

				FINISHED BLOCK SIZE					
			Single dimensions in the cutting chart indicate the size of the cut square (3" = 3" x 3").						
For 2 blocks:			6¼"	7½"	8¾"	10"	12½"	13¾"
Light	A: 1		7⅛"	8⅜"	9⅝"	10⅞"	13⅜"	14⅝"
	B: 1		4"	4⅝"	5¼"	5⅞"	7⅛"	7¾"
	C: 27		1½"	1⅝"	1¾"	1⅞"	2⅛"	2¼"
Dark	D: 3		2¾"	3⅛"	3½"	3⅞"	4⅝"	5"
	E: 21		1½"	1⅝"	1¾"	1⅞"	2⅛"	2¼"

Try this: Use a large-scale medium print instead of a light for A.

Memory

6-Unit Grid

Color Illustration: page 22

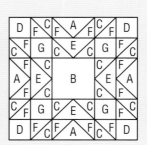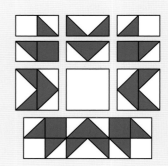

				FINISHED BLOCK SIZE					
			Single dimensions in the cutting chart indicate the size of the cut square (3" = 3" x 3").						
For 1 block:			4½"	6"	7½"	9"	10½"	12"
Light	A: 1		2¾"	3¼"	3¾"	4¼"	4¾"	5¼"
	B: 1		2"	2½"	3"	3½"	4"	4½"
	C: 8		1⅝"	1⅞"	2⅛"	2⅜"	2⅝"	2⅞"
	D: 4		1¼"	1½"	1¾"	2"	2¼"	2½"
Dark	E: 1		2¾"	3¼"	3¾"	4¼"	4¾"	5¼"
	F: 8		1⅝"	1⅞"	2⅛"	2⅜"	2⅝"	2⅞"
	G: 4		1¼"	1½"	1¾"	2"	2¼"	2½"

Try this: Use a medium instead of a light for B.

Light   Light 2   Medium   Medium 2   Dark

Merry Go Round

8-Unit Grid

Color Illustration: page 22

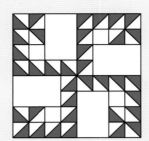
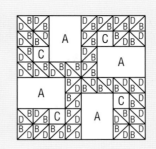
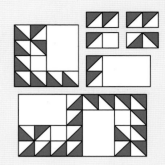

		FINISHED BLOCK SIZE					
		Single dimensions in the cutting chart indicate the size of the cut square (3" = 3" x 3").					
For 1 block:		**6"**	**8"**	**9"**	**10"**	**12"**	**14"**
Light	A: 4 ▭	2" x 2¾"	2½" x 3½"	2¾" x 3⅞"	3" x 4¼"	3½" x 5"	4" x 5¾"
	B: 18 ◱▸◺	1⅝"	1⅞"	2"	2⅛"	2⅜"	2⅝"
	C: 4 ▢	1¼"	1½"	1⅝"	1¾"	2"	2¼"
Dark	D: 18 ◱▸◺	1⅝"	1⅞"	2"	2⅛"	2⅜"	2⅝"

Try this: Use many different darks for D.

Millennium

12-Unit Grid

Color Illustration: page 22

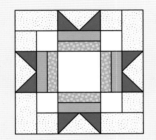
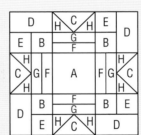
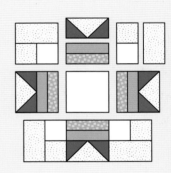

		FINISHED BLOCK SIZE					
		Single dimensions in the cutting chart indicate the size of the cut square (3" = 3" x 3").					
For 1 block:		**6"**	**7½"**	**9"**	**12"**	**13½"**	**15"**
Light	A: 1 ▢	2½"	3"	3½"	4½"	5"	5½"
	B: 4 ▢	1½"	1¾"	2"	2½"	2¾"	3"
Light 2	C: 1 ⊠▸⊠	3¼"	3¾"	4¼"	5¼"	5¾"	6¼"
	D: 4 ▭	1½" x 2½"	1¾" x 3"	2" x 3½"	2½" x 4½"	2¾" x 5"	3" x 5½"
	E: 4 ▢	1½"	1¾"	2"	2½"	2¾"	3"
Medium	F: 4 ▭	1" x 2½"	1⅛" x 3"	1¼" x 3½"	1½" x 4½"	1⅝" x 5"	1¾" x 5½"
Medium 2	G: 4 ▭	1" x 2½"	1⅛" x 3"	1¼" x 3½"	1½" x 4½"	1⅝" x 5"	1¾" x 5½"
Dark	H: 4 ◱▸◺	1⅞"	2⅛"	2⅜"	2⅞"	3⅛"	3⅜"

Try this: Reverse the light and light 2 in every other block.

▢ *Square(s)*   ◱▸◺ *Square(s) cut once diagonally to make half-square triangles*   ⊠▸⊠ *Square(s) cut twice diagonally to make quarter-square triangles*   ▭ *Rectangle(s)*

Minnesota

5-Unit Grid

Color Illustration: page 22

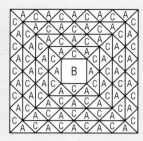

		FINISHED BLOCK SIZE					
		Single dimensions in the cutting chart indicate the size of the cut square (3" = 3" x 3").					
For 1 block:		5"	6¼"	7½"	8¾"	10"	12½"
Light	A: 12 ⊠→⊠	2¼"	2½"	2¾"	3"	3¼"	3¾"
	B: 1 ☐	1½"	1¾"	2"	2¼"	2½"	3"
Dark	C: 12 ⊠→⊠	2¼"	2½"	2¾"	3"	3¼"	3¾"

Try this: Use a medium instead of a light for B.

Mosaic #8

4-Unit Grid

Color Illustration: page 22

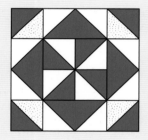
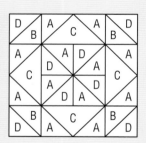
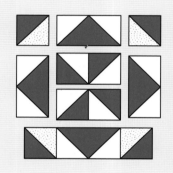

		FINISHED BLOCK SIZE					
		Single dimensions in the cutting chart indicate the size of the cut square (3" = 3" x 3").					
For 1 block:		4"	6"	8"	9"	10"	12"
Light	A: 6 ◺→◺	1⅞"	2⅜"	2⅞"	3⅛"	3⅜"	3⅞"
Light 2	B: 2 ◺→◺	1⅞"	2⅜"	2⅞"	3⅛"	3⅜"	3⅞"
Dark	C: 1 ⊠→⊠	3¼"	4¼"	5¼"	5¾"	6¼"	7¼"
	D: 4 ◺→◺	1⅞"	2⅜"	2⅞"	3⅛"	3⅜"	3⅞"

Try this: Use a medium instead of a dark for C.

☐ Light   ▨ Light 2   ▨ Medium   ▨ Medium 2   ■ Dark

New England Block

5-Unit Grid

Color Illustration: page 22

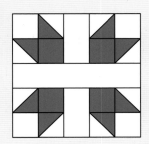 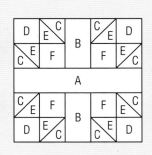 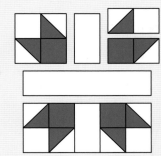

		FINISHED BLOCK SIZE					
		Single dimensions in the cutting chart indicate the size of the cut square (3" = 3" x 3").					
For 1 block:		5"	6¼"	7½"	8¾"	10"	12½"
Light	A: 1 ▭	1½" x 5½"	1¾" x 6¾"	2" x 8"	2¼" x 9¼"	2½" x 10½"	3" x 13"
	B: 2 ▭	1½" x 2½"	1¾" x 3"	2" x 3½"	2¼" x 4"	2½" x 4½"	3" x 5½"
	C: 4 ◲→◺	1⅞"	2⅛"	2⅜"	2⅝"	2⅞"	3⅜"
	D: 4 ☐	1½"	1¾"	2"	2¼"	2½"	3"
Dark	E: 4 ◲→◺	1⅞"	2⅛"	2⅜"	2⅝"	2⅞"	3⅜"
	F: 4 ☐	1½"	1¾"	2"	2¼"	2½"	3"

Try this: Use a different dark in every quadrant of the block.

New Waterwheel

9-Unit Grid

Color Illustration: page 22

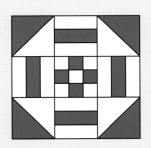 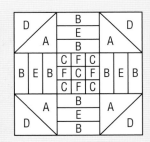 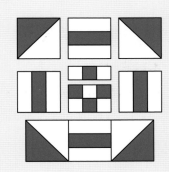

		FINISHED BLOCK SIZE					
		Single dimensions in the cutting chart indicate the size of the cut square (3" = 3" x 3").					
For 1 block:		6¾"	9"	10⅛"	11¼"	12⅜"	13½"
Light	A: 2 ◲→◺	3⅛"	3⅞"	4¼"	4⅝"	5"	5⅜"
	B: 8 ▭	1¼" x 2¾"	1½" x 3½"	1⅝" x 3⅞"	1¾" x 4¼"	1⅞" x 4⅝"	2" x 5"
	C: 5 ☐	1¼"	1½"	1⅝"	1¾"	1⅞"	2"
Dark	D: 2 ◲→◺	3⅛"	3⅞"	4¼"	4⅝"	5"	5⅜"
	E: 4 ▭	1¼" x 2¾"	1½" x 3½"	1⅝" x 3⅞"	1¾" x 4¼"	1⅞" x 4⅝"	2" x 5"
	F: 4 ☐	1¼"	1½"	1⅝"	1¾"	1⅞"	2"

Try this: Reverse the lights and darks.

☐ Square(s)   ◲→◺ Square(s) cut once diagonally to make half-square triangles   ⊠→⧄ Square(s) cut twice diagonally to make quarter-square triangles   ▭ Rectangle(s)

Nine Patch Straight Furrow

3-Unit Grid

Color Illustration: page 23

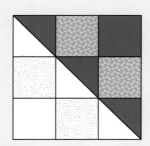
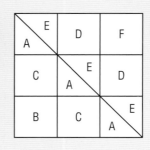
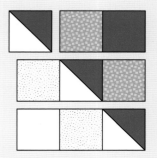

FINISHED BLOCK SIZE

Single dimensions in the cutting chart indicate the size of the cut square (3" = 3" x 3").

For 2 blocks:			4½"	6"	7½"	9"	10½"	12"
Light	A: 3		2⅜"	2⅞"	3⅜"	3⅞"	4⅜"	4⅞"
	B: 2		2"	2½"	3"	3½"	4"	4½"
Light 2	C: 4		2"	2½"	3"	3½"	4"	4½"
Medium	D: 4		2"	2½"	3"	3½"	4"	4½"
Dark	E: 3		2⅜"	2⅞"	3⅜"	3⅞"	4⅜"	4⅞"
	F: 2		2"	2½"	3"	3½"	4"	4½"

Try this: Use a different combination of fabrics for each block.

The North Carolina Beauty

5-Unit Grid

Color Illustration: page 23

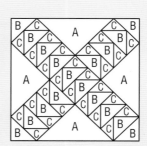

FINISHED BLOCK SIZE

Single dimensions in the cutting chart indicate the size of the cut square (3" = 3" x 3").

For 1 block:			5"	6¼"	7½"	8¾"	10"	12½"
Light	A: 1		4¼"	5"	5¾"	6½"	7¼"	8¾"
	B: 9		1⅞"	2⅛"	2⅜"	2⅝"	2⅞"	3⅜"
Dark	C: 7		2¼"	2½"	2¾"	3"	3¼"	3¾"

Try this: Use one light for A and a different light for B.

☐ Light   ☐ Light 2   ▨ Medium   ▨ Medium 2   ■ Dark

Old Grey Goose

4-Unit Grid

Color Illustration: page 23

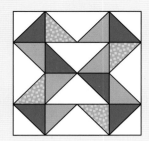
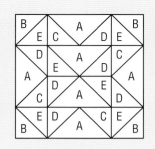
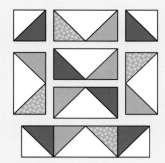

FINISHED BLOCK SIZE
Single dimensions in the cutting chart indicate the size of the cut square (3" = 3" x 3").

For 2 blocks:			4"	6"	8"	9"	10"	12"
Light	A: 3	⊠→⊠	3¼"	4¼"	5¼"	5¾"	6¼"	7¼"
	B: 4	◻→◹	1⅞"	2⅜"	2⅞"	3⅛"	3⅜"	3⅞"
Medium	C: 4	◻→◹	1⅞"	2⅜"	2⅞"	3⅛"	3⅜"	3⅞"
Medium 2	D: 6	◻→◹	1⅞"	2⅜"	2⅞"	3⅛"	3⅜"	3⅞"
Dark	E: 6	◻→◹	1⅞"	2⅜"	2⅞"	3⅛"	3⅜"	3⅞"

Try this: Use a scrappy assortment of mediums and darks for C, D, and E.

On the Square

9-Unit Grid

Color Illustration: page 23

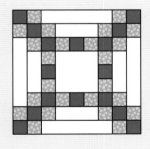
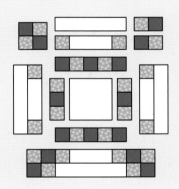

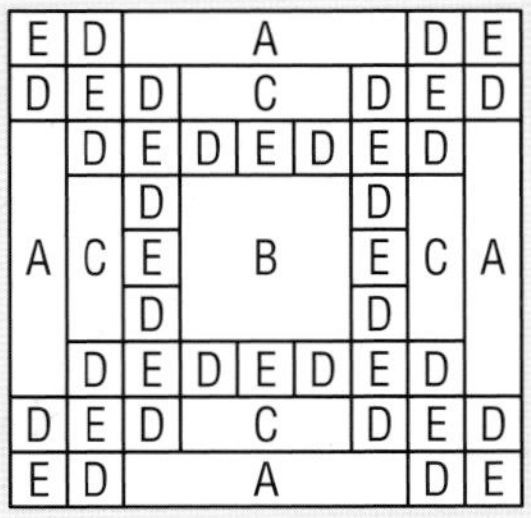

FINISHED BLOCK SIZE
Single dimensions in the cutting chart indicate the size of the cut square (3" = 3" x 3").

For 1 block:			6¾"	9"	10⅛"	11¼"	12⅜"	13½"
Light	A: 4	▭	1¼" x 4¼"	1½" x 5½"	1⅝" x 6⅛"	1¾" x 6¾"	1⅞" x 7⅜"	2" x 8"
	B: 1	◻	2¾"	3½"	3⅞"	4¼"	4⅝"	5"
	C: 4	▭	1¼" x 2¾"	1½" x 3½"	1⅝" x 3⅞"	1¾" x 4¼"	1⅞" x 4⅝"	2" x 5"
Medium	D: 24	◻	1¼"	1½"	1⅝"	1¾"	1⅞"	2"
Dark	E: 16	◻	1¼"	1½"	1⅝"	1¾"	1⅞"	2"

Try this: Reverse the lights and darks.

◻ *Square(s)*   ◻→◹ *Square(s) cut once diagonally to make half-square triangles*   ⊠→⊠ *Square(s) cut twice diagonally to make quarter-square triangles*   ▭ *Rectangle(s)*

One More Block

6-Unit Grid

Color Illustration: page 23

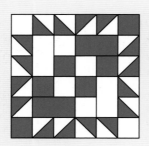
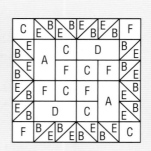
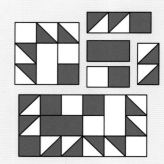

FINISHED BLOCK SIZE

Single dimensions in the cutting chart indicate the size of the cut square (3" = 3" x 3").

For 1 block:			4½"	6"	7½"	9"	10½"	12"
Light	A: 2		1¼" x 2"	1½" x 2½"	1¾" x 3"	2" x 3½"	2¼" x 4"	2½" x 4½"
	B: 8		1⅝"	1⅞"	2⅛"	2⅜"	2⅝"	2⅞"
	C: 6		1¼"	1½"	1¾"	2"	2¼"	2½"
Dark	D: 2		1¼" x 2"	1½" x 2½"	1¾" x 3"	2" x 3½"	2¼" x 4"	2½" x 4½"
	E: 8		1⅝"	1⅞"	2⅛"	2⅜"	2⅝"	2⅞"
	F: 6		1¼"	1½"	1¾"	2"	2¼"	2½"

Try this: Use a different combination of lights and darks in each quadrant of the block.

Our Editor

4-Unit Grid

Color Illustration: page 23

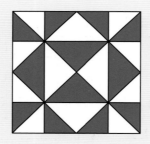
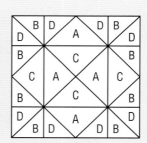

FINISHED BLOCK SIZE

Single dimensions in the cutting chart indicate the size of the cut square (3" = 3" x 3").

For 1 block:			4"	6"	8"	9"	10"	12"
Light	A: 1		3¼"	4¼"	5¼"	5¾"	6¼"	7¼"
	B: 4		1⅞"	2⅜"	2⅞"	3⅛"	3⅜"	3⅞"
Dark	C: 1		3¼"	4¼"	5¼"	5¾"	6¼"	7¼"
	D: 4		1⅞"	2⅜"	2⅞"	3⅛"	3⅜"	3⅞"

Try this: Use a medium instead of a light for A.

Light Light 2 Medium Medium 2 Dark

The Ozark Trail

10-Unit Grid

Color Illustration: page 23

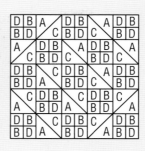
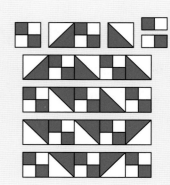

		FINISHED BLOCK SIZE					
		Single dimensions in the cutting chart indicate the size of the cut square (3" = 3" x 3").					
For 1 block:		6¼"	7½"	8¾"	10"	12½"	13¾"
Light	A: 6	2⅛"	2⅜"	2⅝"	2⅞"	3⅜"	3⅝"
	B: 26	1⅛"	1¼"	1⅜"	1½"	1¾"	1⅞"
Dark	C: 6	2⅛"	2⅜"	2⅝"	2⅞"	3⅜"	3⅝"
	D: 26	1⅛"	1¼"	1⅜"	1½"	1¾"	1⅞"

Try this: Use one light for A and a different light or a medium for B.

Pennsylvania

6-Unit Grid

Color Illustration: page 23

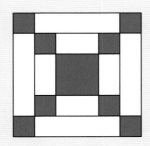
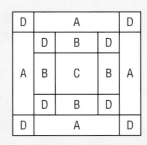
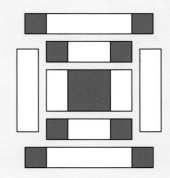

		FINISHED BLOCK SIZE					
		Single dimensions in the cutting chart indicate the size of the cut square (3" = 3" x 3").					
For 1 block:		4½"	6"	7½"	9"	10½"	12"
Light	A: 4	1¼" x 3½"	1½" x 4½"	1¾" x 5½"	2" x 6½"	2¼" x 7½"	2½" x 8½"
	B: 4	1¼" x 2"	1½" x 2½"	1¾" x 3"	2" x 3½"	2¼" x 4"	2½" x 4½"
Dark	C: 1	2"	2½"	3"	3½"	4"	4½"
	D: 8	1¼"	1½"	1¾"	2"	2¼"	2½"

Try this: Use a pictorial print for C.

| ☐ Square(s) | ◺→◹ Square(s) cut once diagonally to make half-square triangles | ⊠→⧖ Square(s) cut twice diagonally to make quarter-square triangles | ▭ Rectangle(s) |

Perkiomen Valley

3-Unit Grid

Color Illustration: page 23

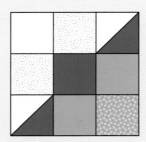
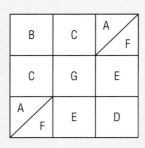
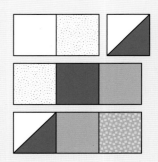

		FINISHED BLOCK SIZE					
		Single dimensions in the cutting chart indicate the size of the cut square (3" = 3" x 3").					
For 1 block:		4½"	6"	7½"	9"	10½"	12"
Light	A: 1 ◻→◹	2⅜"	2⅞"	3⅜"	3⅞"	4⅜"	4⅞"
	B: 1 ◻	2"	2½"	3"	3½"	4"	4½"
Light 2	C: 2 ◻	2"	2½"	3"	3½"	4"	4½"
Medium	D: 1 ◻	2"	2½"	3"	3½"	4"	4½"
Medium 2	E: 2 ◻	2"	2½"	3"	3½"	4"	4½"
Dark	F: 1 ◻→◹	2⅜"	2⅞"	3⅜"	3⅞"	4⅜"	4⅞"
	G: 1 ◻	2"	2½"	3"	3½"	4"	4½"

Try this: Use a scrappy assortment of lights and mediums for A–E.

Philadelphia Pavement

5-Unit Grid

Color Illustration: page 23

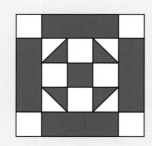
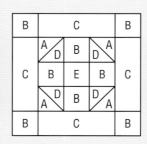
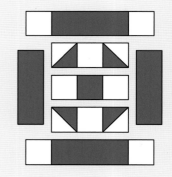

		FINISHED BLOCK SIZE					
		Single dimensions in the cutting chart indicate the size of the cut square (3" = 3" x 3").					
For 1 block:		5"	6¼"	7½"	8¾"	10"	12½"
Light	A: 2 ◻→◹	1⅞"	2⅛"	2⅜"	2⅝"	2⅞"	3⅜"
	B: 8 ◻	1½"	1¾"	2"	2¼"	2½"	3"
Dark	C: 4 ▭	1½" x 3½"	1¾" x 4¼"	2" x 5"	2¼" x 5¾"	2½" x 6½"	3" x 8"
	D: 2 ◻→◹	1⅞"	2⅛"	2⅜"	2⅝"	2⅞"	3⅜"
	E: 1 ◻	1½"	1¾"	2"	2¼"	2½"	3"

Try this: Reverse the lights and darks in every other block.

96

Picket Fence

6-Unit Grid

Color Illustration: page 23

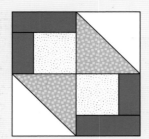 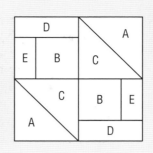 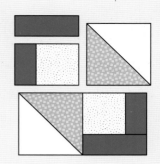

FINISHED BLOCK SIZE						
Single dimensions in the cutting chart indicate the size of the cut square (3" = 3" x 3")						
For 1 block:	**4½"**	**6"**	**7½"**	**9"**	**10½"**	**12"**
Light A: 1	3⅛"	3⅞"	4⅝"	5⅜"	6⅛"	6⅞"
Light 2 B: 2	2"	2½"	3"	3½"	4"	4½"
Medium C: 1	3⅛"	3⅞"	4⅝"	5⅜"	6⅛"	6⅞"
Dark: D: 2	1¼" x 2¾"	1½" x 3½"	1¾" x 4¼"	2" x 5"	2¼" x 5¾"	2½" x 6½"
E: 2	1¼" x 2"	1½" x 2½"	1¾" x 3"	2" x 3½"	2¼" x 4"	2½" x 4½"

Try this: Use a different medium in every block.

Pine Burr

10-Unit Grid

Color Illustration: page 23

 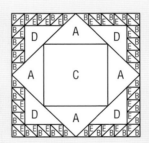 

FINISHED BLOCK SIZE						
Single dimensions in the cutting chart indicate the size of the cut square (3" = 3" x 3").						
For 1 block:	**6¼"**	**7½"**	**8¾"**	**10"**	**12½"**	**13¾"**
Light A: 1	4⅜"	5"	5⅝"	6¼"	7½"	8⅛"
B: 18	1½"	1⅝"	1¾"	1⅞"	2⅛"	2¼"
Medium C: 1	3⅝"	4¼"	4⅞"	5½"	6¾"	7⅜"
D: 2	2¾"	3⅛"	3½"	3⅞"	4⅝"	5"
Dark E: 14	1½"	1⅝"	1¾"	1⅞"	2⅛"	2¼"

Try this: Use a large-scale print for C and D.

⬜ *Square(s)*   ◺→◿ *Square(s) cut once diagonally to make half-square triangles*   ⊠→⊠ *Square(s) cut twice diagonally to make quarter-square triangles*   ▭ *Rectangle(s)*

97

Plaid

5-Unit Grid

Color Illustration: page 24

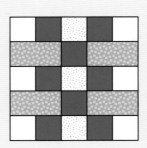

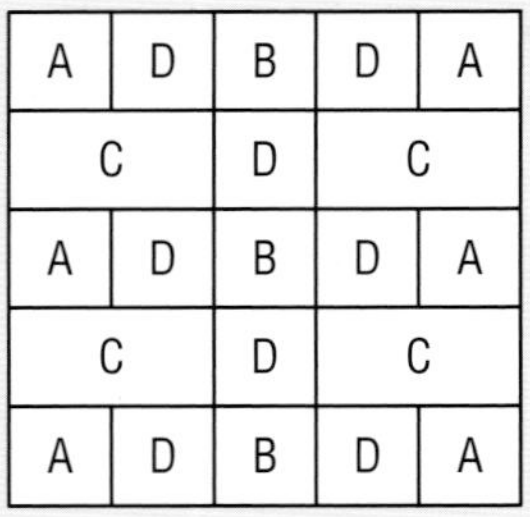

A	D	B	D	A
C		D		C
A	D	B	D	A
C		D		C
A	D	B	D	A

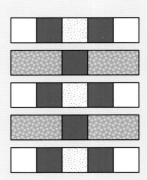

FINISHED BLOCK SIZE
Single dimensions in the cutting chart indicate the size of the cut square (3" = 3" x 3").

For 1 block:		5"	6¼"	7½"	8¾"	10"	12½"
Light	A: 6 ☐	1½"	1¾"	2"	2¼"	2½"	3"
Light 2	B: 3 ☐	1½"	1¾"	2"	2¼"	2½"	3"
Medium	C: 4 ▭	1½" x 2½"	1¾" x 3"	2" x 3½"	2¼" x 4"	2½" x 4½"	3" x 5½"
Dark	D: 8 ☐	1½"	1¾"	2"	2¼"	2½"	3"

Try this: Reverse the mediums and darks.

A Plain Block

4-Unit Grid

Color Illustration: page 24

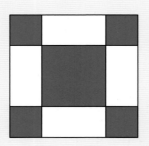

C	A	C
A	B	A
C	A	C

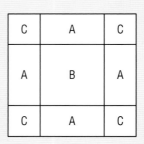 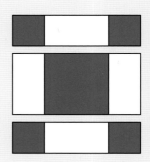

FINISHED BLOCK SIZE
Single dimensions in the cutting chart indicate the size of the cut square (3" = 3" x 3").

For 1 block:		4"	6"	8"	9"	10"	12"
Light	A: 4 ▭	1½" x 2½"	2" x 3½"	2½" x 4½"	2¾" x 5"	3" x 5½"	3½" x 6½"
Dark	B: 1 ☐	2½"	3½"	4½"	5"	5½"	6½"
	C: 4 ☐	1½"	2"	2½"	2¾"	3"	3½"

Try this: Reverse the lights and darks in every other block.

☐ *Light*	▦ *Light 2*	▨ *Medium*	▩ *Medium 2*	■ *Dark*

Practical Orchard

3-Unit Grid

Color Illustration: page 24

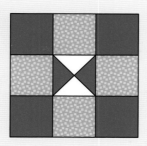

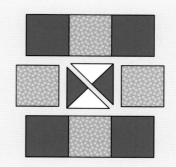

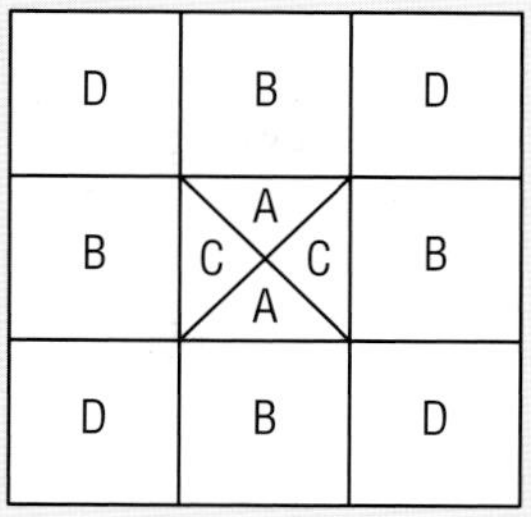

	FINISHED BLOCK SIZE					
	Single dimensions in the cutting chart indicate the size of the cut square (3" = 3" x 3").					
For 2 blocks:	4½"	6"	7½"	9"	10½"	12"
Light A: 1 ⊠→⊠	2¾"	3¼"	3¾"	4¼"	4¾"	5¼"
Medium B: 8 ☐	2"	2½"	3"	3½"	4"	4½"
Dark C: 1 ⊠→⊠	2¾"	3¼"	3¾"	4¼"	4¾"	5¼"
D: 8 ☐	2"	2½"	3"	3½"	4"	4½"

Try this: Reverse the darks and mediums in every other block.

Practical Orchard II

3-Unit Grid

Color Illustration: page 24

Note: *This block is identical to Hour Glass #2 (page 80) in size, shape, and position of the pieces, but the value arrangement is different.*

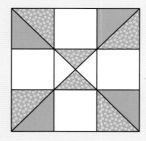

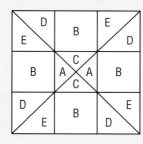

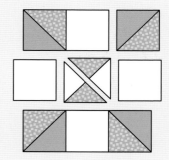

	FINISHED BLOCK SIZE					
	Single dimensions in the cutting chart indicate the size of the cut square (3" = 3" x 3").					
For 2 blocks:	4½"	6"	7½"	9"	10½"	12"
Light A: 1 ⊠→⊠	2¾"	3¼"	3¾"	4¼"	4¾"	5¼"
B: 8 ☐	2"	2½"	3"	3½"	4"	4½"
Medium C: 1 ⊠→⊠	2¾"	3¼"	3¾"	4¼"	4¾"	5¼"
D: 4 ◺→◺	2⅜"	2⅞"	3⅜"	3⅞"	4⅜"	4⅞"
Medium 2 E: 4 ◺→◺	2⅜"	2⅞"	3⅜"	3⅞"	4⅜"	4⅞"

Try this: Use one light for A and a different light for B.

Square(s)	Square(s) cut once diagonally to make half-square triangles	⊠→⊠ Square(s) cut twice diagonally to make quarter-square triangles	Rectangle(s)

Premium Star

10-Unit Grid

Color Illustration: page 24

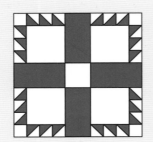
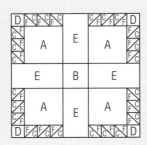
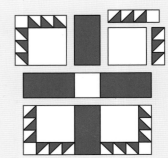

		FINISHED BLOCK SIZE					
		Single dimensions in the cutting chart indicate the size of the cut square (3" = 3" x 3").					
For 1 block:		6¼"	7½"	8¾"	10"	12½"	13¾"
Light	A: 4 ☐	2⅜"	2¾"	3⅛"	3½"	4¼"	4⅝"
	B: 1 ☐	1¾"	2"	2¼"	2½"	3"	3¼"
	C: 12 ◺▸◹	1½"	1⅝"	1¾"	1⅞"	2⅛"	2¼"
	D: 4 ☐	1⅛"	1¼"	1⅜"	1½"	1¾"	1⅞"
Dark	E: 4 ▭	1¾" x 3"	2" x 3½"	2¼" x 4"	2½" x 4½"	3" x 5½"	3¼" x 6"
	F: 12 ◺▸◹	1½"	1⅝"	1¾"	1⅞"	2⅛"	2¼"

Try this: Reverse the lights and darks.

The Presidential Armchair

9-Unit Grid

Color Illustration: page 24

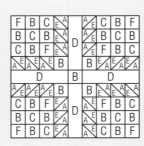

		FINISHED BLOCK SIZE					
		Single dimensions in the cutting chart indicate the size of the cut square (3" = 3" x 3").					
For 1 block:		6¾"	9"	10⅛"	11¼"	12⅜"	13½"
Light	A: 12 ◺▸◹	1⅝"	1⅞"	2"	2⅛"	2¼"	2⅜"
	B: 21 ☐	1¼"	1½"	1⅝"	1¾"	1⅞"	2"
Medium	C: 12 ☐	1¼"	1½"	1⅝"	1¾"	1⅞"	2"
Medium 2	D: 4 ▭	1¼" x 3½"	1½" x 4½"	1⅝" x 5"	1¾" x 5½"	1⅞" x 6"	2" x 6½"
Dark	E: 12 ◺▸◹	1⅝"	1⅞"	2"	2⅛"	2¼"	2⅜"
	F: 8 ☐	1¼"	1½"	1⅝"	1¾"	1⅞"	2"

Try this: Use a different combination of darks and mediums in every quadrant of the block.

☐ Light   ▨ Light 2   ▨ Medium   ▨ Medium 2   ■ Dark

Proof through the Night

3-Unit Grid

Color Illustration: page 24

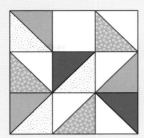
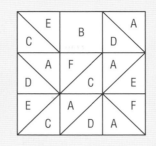
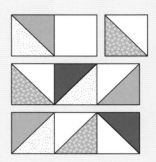

	FINISHED BLOCK SIZE					
	Single dimensions in the cutting chart indicate the size of the cut square (3" = 3" x 3").					
For 2 blocks:	4½"	6"	7½"	9"	10½"	12"
Light — A: 5 ☐→◩	2⅜"	2⅞"	3⅜"	3⅞"	4⅜"	4⅞"
B: 2 ☐	2"	2½"	3"	3½"	4"	4½"
Light 2 — C: 3 ☐→◩	2⅜"	2⅞"	3⅜"	3⅞"	4⅜"	4⅞"
Medium — D: 3 ☐→◩	2⅜"	2⅞"	3⅜"	3⅞"	4⅜"	4⅞"
Medium 2 — E: 3 ☐→◩	2⅜"	2⅞"	3⅜"	3⅞"	4⅜"	4⅞"
Dark — F: 2 ☐→◩	2⅜"	2⅞"	3⅜"	3⅞"	4⅜"	4⅞"

Try this: Use a scrappy assortment of fabrics for C, D, and E.

Propeller

5-Unit Grid

Color Illustration: page 24

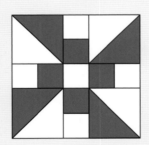
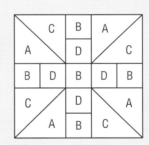
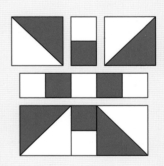

	FINISHED BLOCK SIZE					
	Single dimensions in the cutting chart indicate the size of the cut square (3" = 3" x 3").					
For 1 block:	5"	6¼"	7½"	8¾"	10"	12½"
Light — A: 2 ☐→◩	2⅞"	3⅜"	3⅞"	4⅜"	4⅞"	5⅞"
B: 5 ☐	1½"	1¾"	2"	2¼"	2½"	3"
Dark — C: 2 ☐→◩	2⅞"	3⅜"	3⅞"	4⅜"	4⅞"	5⅞"
D: 4 ☐	1½"	1¾"	2"	2¼"	2½"	3"

Try this: Use a medium instead of a dark for C.

☐ Square(s)	◩ Square(s) cut once diagonally to make half-square triangles	⊠ Square(s) cut twice diagonally to make quarter-square triangles
		▭ Rectangle(s)

Providence

5-Unit Grid

Color Illustration: page 24

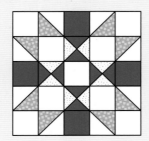
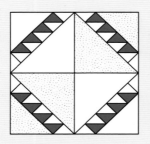
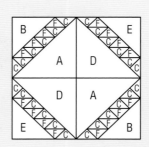
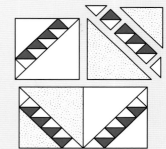

		FINISHED BLOCK SIZE					
		Single dimensions in the cutting chart indicate the size of the cut square (3" = 3" x 3").					
For 1 block:		5"	6¼"	7½"	8¾"	10"	12½"
Light	A: 4 ▢→◪	1⅞"	2⅛"	2⅜"	2⅝"	2⅞"	3⅜"
	B: 9 ▢	1½"	1¾"	2"	2¼"	2½"	3"
Light 2	C: 2 ⊠→⊠	2¼"	2½"	2¾"	3"	3¼"	3¾"
Medium	D: 4 ▢→◪	1⅞"	2⅛"	2⅜"	2⅝"	2⅞"	3⅜"
Dark	E: 2 ⊠→⊠	2¼"	2½"	2¾"	3"	3¼"	3¾"
	F: 4 ▢	1½"	1¾"	2"	2¼"	2½"	3"

Try this: Reverse light 2 and the dark.

Puffin Beaks

6-Unit Grid

Color Illustration: page 24

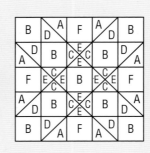
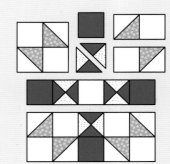

		FINISHED BLOCK SIZE					
		Single dimensions in the cutting chart indicate the size of the cut square (3" = 3" x 3").					
For 1 block:		4½"	6"	7½"	9"	10½"	12"
Light	A: 1 ▢→◪	3⅛"	3⅞"	4⅝"	5⅜"	6⅛"	6⅞"
	B: 1 ▢→◪	2⅜"	2⅞"	3⅜"	3⅞"	4⅜"	4⅞"
	C: 6 ⊠→⊠	2"	2¼"	2½"	2¾"	3"	3¼"
Light 2	D: 1 ▢→◪	3⅛"	3⅞"	4⅝"	5⅜"	6⅛"	6⅞"
	E: 1 ▢→◪	2⅜"	2⅞"	3⅜"	3⅞"	4⅜"	4⅞"
Dark	F: 4 ⊠→⊠	2"	2¼"	2½"	2¾"	3"	3¼"

Try this: Use a medium instead of light 2 in every other block.

□ Light   ▨ Light 2   ▨ Medium   ▨ Medium 2   ■ Dark

Puss in the Corner II

5-Unit Grid

Color Illustration: page 24

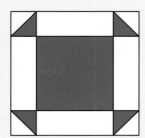
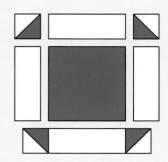

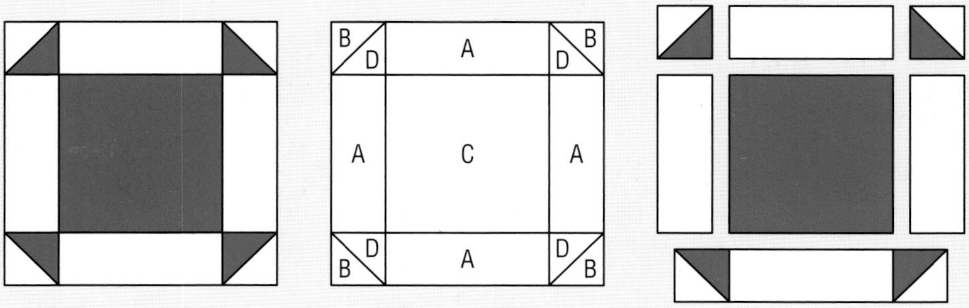

		FINISHED BLOCK SIZE					
		Single dimensions in the cutting chart indicate the size of the cut square (3" = 3" x 3").					
For 1 block:		5"	6¼"	7½"	8¾"	10"	12½"
Light	A: 4 ▭	1½" x 3½"	1¾" x 4¼"	2" x 5"	2¼" x 5¾"	2½" x 6½"	3" x 8"
	B: 2 ◩→◩	1⅞"	2⅛"	2⅜"	2⅝"	2⅞"	3⅜"
Dark	C: 1 ▢	3½"	4¼"	5"	5¾"	6½"	8"
	D: 2 ◩→◩	1⅞"	2⅛"	2⅜"	2⅝"	2⅞"	3⅜"

Try this: Use a large-scale print for C.

Raven Chase

4-Unit Grid

Color Illustration: page 24

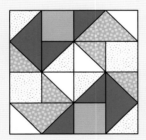
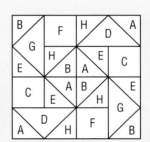
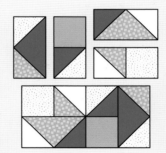

		FINISHED BLOCK SIZE					
		Single dimensions in the cutting chart indicate the size of the cut square (3" = 3" x 3").					
For 2 blocks:		4"	6"	8"	9"	10"	12"
Light	A: 4 ◩→◩	1⅞"	2⅜"	2⅞"	3⅛"	3⅜"	3⅞"
Light 2	B: 4 ◩→◩	1⅞"	2⅜"	2⅞"	3⅛"	3⅜"	3⅞"
	C: 4 ▢	1½"	2"	2½"	2¾"	3"	3½"
Medium	D: 1 ⊠→⊠	3¼"	4¼"	5¼"	5¾"	6¼"	7¼"
	E: 4 ◩→◩	1⅞"	2⅜"	2⅞"	3⅛"	3⅜"	3⅞"
Medium 2	F: 4 ▢	1½"	2"	2½"	2¾"	3"	3½"
Dark	G: 1 ⊠→⊠	3¼"	4¼"	5¼"	5¾"	6¼"	7¼"
	H: 4 ◩→◩	1⅞"	2⅜"	2⅞"	3⅛"	3⅜"	3⅞"

Try this: Use a light instead of medium 2 for F.

▭ *Square(s)*   ◩→◩ *Square(s) cut once diagonally to make half-square triangles*   ⊠→⊠ *Square(s) cut twice diagonally to make quarter-square triangles*   ▭ *Rectangle(s)*

103

Red Cross II

5-Unit Grid

Color Illustration: page 25

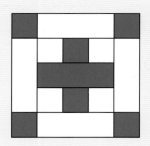

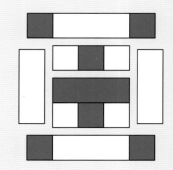

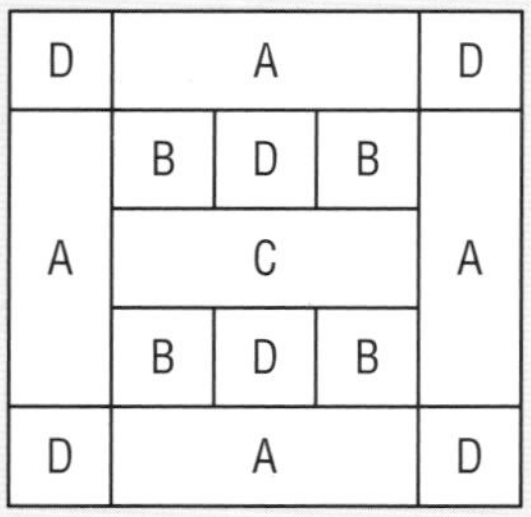

		FINISHED BLOCK SIZE					
		Single dimensions in the cutting chart indicate the size of the cut square (3" = 3" x 3").					
For 1 block:		5"	6¼"	7½"	8¾"	10"	12½"
Light	A: 4	1½" x 3½"	1¾" x 4¼"	2" x 5"	2¼" x 5¾"	2½" x 6½"	3" x 8"
	B: 4	1½"	1¾"	2"	2¼"	2½"	3"
Dark	C: 1	1½" x 3½"	1¾" x 4¼"	2" x 5"	2¼" x 5¾"	2½" x 6½"	3" x 8"
	D: 6	1½"	1¾"	2"	2¼"	2½"	3"

Try this: Use a different light or a medium for B.

Red Cross III

5-Unit Grid

Color Illustration: page 25

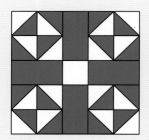

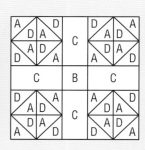

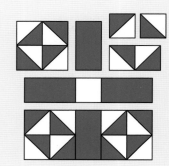

		FINISHED BLOCK SIZE					
		Single dimensions in the cutting chart indicate the size of the cut square (3" = 3" x 3").					
For 1 block:		5"	6¼"	7½"	8¾"	10"	12½"
Light	A: 8	1⅞"	2⅛"	2⅜"	2⅝"	2⅞"	3⅜"
	B: 1	1½"	1¾"	2"	2¼"	2½"	3"
Dark	C: 4	1½" x 2½"	1¾" x 3"	2" x 3½"	2¼" x 4"	2½" x 4½"	3" x 5½"
	D: 8	1⅞"	2⅛"	2⅜"	2⅝"	2⅞"	3⅜"

Try this: Use a medium instead of a dark for C.

Light   Light 2   Medium   Medium 2   Dark

Remember Me

2-Unit Grid

Color Illustration: page 25

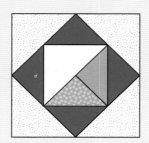 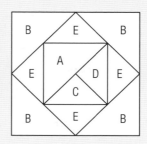 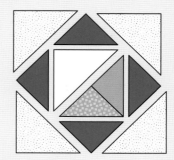

	FINISHED BLOCK SIZE
	Single dimensions in the cutting chart indicate the size of the cut square (3" = 3" x 3").

For 4 blocks:		4"	6"	8"	9"	10"	12"
Light	A: 2 ◻→◹	2⅞"	3⅞"	4⅞"	5⅜"	5⅞"	6⅞"
Light 2	B: 8 ◻→◹	2⅞"	3⅞"	4⅞"	5⅜"	5⅞"	6⅞"
Medium	C: 1 ⊠→⧅	3¼"	4¼"	5¼"	5¾"	6¼"	7¼"
Medium 2	D: 1 ⊠→⧅	3¼"	4¼"	5¼"	5¾"	6¼"	7¼"
Dark	E: 4 ⊠→⧅	3¼"	4¼"	5¼"	5¾"	6¼"	7¼"

Try this: Use a different combination of fabrics in every block.

Ribbon Quilt

3-Unit Grid

Color Illustration: page 25

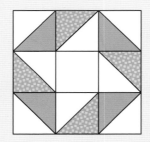 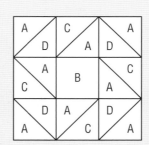 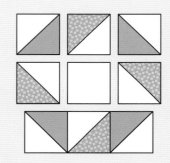

	FINISHED BLOCK SIZE
	Single dimensions in the cutting chart indicate the size of the cut square (3" = 3" x 3").

For 1 block:		4½"	6"	7½"	9"	10½"	12"
Light	A: 4 ◻→◹	2⅜"	2⅞"	3⅜"	3⅞"	4⅜"	4⅞"
	B: 1 ◻	2"	2½"	3"	3½"	4"	4½"
Medium	C: 2 ◻→◹	2⅜"	2⅞"	3⅜"	3⅞"	4⅜"	4⅞"
Medium 2	D: 2 ◻→◹	2⅜"	2⅞"	3⅜"	3⅞"	4⅜"	4⅞"

Try this: Use one light for A and a different light for B.

◻ *Square(s)* ◻→◹ *Square(s) cut once diagonally to make half-square triangles* ⊠→⧅ *Square(s) cut twice diagonally to make quarter-square triangles* ▭ *Rectangle(s)*

Road to the White House

6-Unit Grid

Color Illustration: page 25

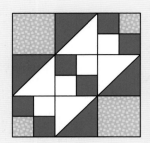
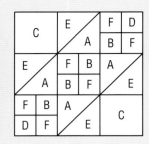
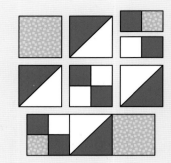

		FINISHED BLOCK SIZE					
		Single dimensions in the cutting chart indicate the size of the cut square (3" = 3" x 3").					
For 1 block:		4½"	6"	7½"	9"	10½"	12"
Light	A: 2 ☐→◩	2⅜"	2⅞"	3⅜"	3⅞"	4⅜"	4⅞"
	B: 4 ☐	1¼"	1½"	1¾"	2"	2¼"	2½"
Medium	C: 2 ☐	2"	2½"	3"	3½"	4"	4½"
	D: 2 ☐	1¼"	1½"	1¾"	2"	2¼"	2½"
Dark	E: 2 ☐→◩	2⅜"	2⅞"	3⅜"	3⅞"	4⅜"	4⅞"
	F: 6 ☐	1¼"	1½"	1¾"	2"	2¼"	2½"

Try this: Use a different medium in every block.

Rocky Road to California

6-Unit Grid

Color Illustration: page 25

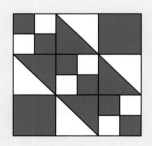
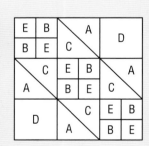
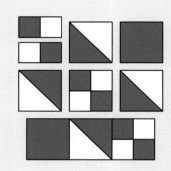

		FINISHED BLOCK SIZE					
		Single dimensions in the cutting chart indicate the size of the cut square (3" = 3" x 3").					
For 1 block:		4½"	6"	7½"	9"	10½"	12"
Light	A: 2 ☐→◩	2⅜"	2⅞"	3⅜"	3⅞"	4⅜"	4⅞"
	B: 6 ☐	1¼"	1½"	1¾"	2"	2¼"	2½"
Dark	C: 2 ☐→◩	2⅜"	2⅞"	3⅜"	3⅞"	4⅜"	4⅞"
	D: 2 ☐	2"	2½"	3"	3½"	4"	4½"
	E: 6 ☐	1¼"	1½"	1¾"	2"	2¼"	2½"

Try this: Use a medium instead of a dark for D and E.

☐ Light ▦ Light 2 ▨ Medium ▩ Medium 2 ■ Dark

Rocky Road to Dublin

6-Unit Grid

Color Illustration: page 25

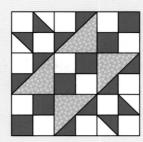
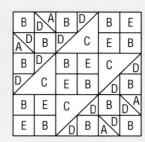
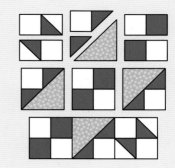

		FINISHED BLOCK SIZE					
		Single dimensions in the cutting chart indicate the size of the cut square (3" = 3" x 3").					
For 1 block:		4½"	6"	7½"	9"	10½"	12"
Light	A: 2 ◹▸◸	1⅝"	1⅞"	2⅛"	2⅜"	2⅝"	2⅞"
	B: 14 ☐	1¼"	1½"	1¾"	2"	2¼"	2½"
Medium	C: 2 ◹▸◸	2⅜"	2⅞"	3⅜"	3⅞"	4⅜"	4⅞"
Dark	D: 6 ◹▸◸	1⅝"	1⅞"	2⅛"	2⅜"	2⅝"	2⅞"
	E: 6 ☐	1¼"	1½"	1¾"	2"	2¼"	2½"

Try this: Use one light for A and a different light for B.

Rolling Nine Patch

5-Unit Grid

Color Illustration: page 25

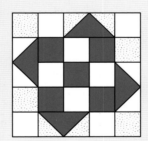
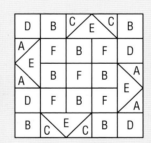
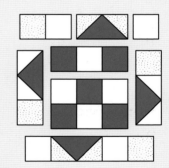

		FINISHED BLOCK SIZE					
		Single dimensions in the cutting chart indicate the size of the cut square (3" = 3" x 3").					
For 1 block:		5"	6¼"	7½"	8¾"	10"	12½"
Light	A: 2 ◹▸◸	1⅞"	2⅛"	2⅜"	2⅝"	2⅞"	3⅜"
	B: 8 ☐	1½"	1¾"	2"	2¼"	2½"	3"
Light 2	C: 2 ◹▸◸	1⅞"	2⅛"	2⅜"	2⅝"	2⅞"	3⅜"
	D: 4 ☐	1½"	1¾"	2"	2¼"	2½"	3"
Dark	E: 1 ⊠▸⊠	3¼"	3¾"	4¼"	4¾"	5¼"	6¼"
	F: 5 ☐	1½"	1¾"	2"	2¼"	2½"	3"

Try this: Use a different combination of fabrics in every block.

☐ Square(s)   ◹▸◸ Square(s) cut once diagonally to make half-square triangles   ⊠▸⊠ Square(s) cut twice diagonally to make quarter-square triangles   ▭ Rectangle(s)

Rolling Pinwheel

6-Unit Grid

Color Illustration: page 25

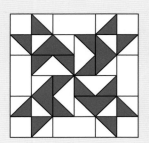
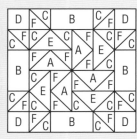
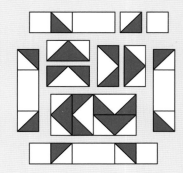

FINISHED BLOCK SIZE

Single dimensions in the cutting chart indicate the size of the cut square (3" = 3" x 3").

For 1 block:		4½"	6"	7½"	9"	10½"	12"
Light	A: 1 ⊠→⧖	2¾"	3¼"	3¾"	4¼"	4¾"	5¼"
	B: 4 ▭	1¼" x 2"	1½" x 2½"	1¾" x 3"	2" x 3½"	2¼" x 4"	2½" x 4½"
	C: 8 ◹→◺	1⅝"	1⅞"	2⅛"	2⅜"	2⅝"	2⅞"
	D: 4 ▢	1¼"	1½"	1¾"	2"	2¼"	2½"
Dark	E: 1 ⊠→⧖	2¾"	3¼"	3¾"	4¼"	4¾"	5¼"
	F: 8 ◹→◺	1⅝"	1⅞"	2⅛"	2⅜"	2⅝"	2⅞"

Try this: Reverse the lights and darks.

The Rosebud

8-Unit Grid

Color Illustration: page 25

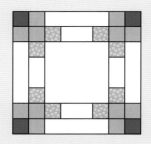
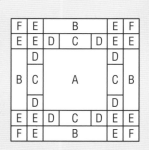
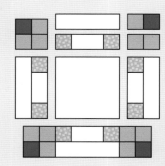

FINISHED BLOCK SIZE

Single dimensions in the cutting chart indicate the size of the cut square (3" = 3" x 3").

For 1 block:		6"	8"	9"	10"	12"	14"
Light	A: 1 ▢	3½"	4½"	5"	5½"	6½"	7½"
	B: 4 ▭	1¼" x 3½"	1½" x 4½"	1⅝" x 5"	1¾" x 5½"	2" x 6½"	2¼" x 7½"
	C: 4 ▭	1¼" x 2"	1½" x 2½"	1⅝" x 2¾"	1¾" x 3"	2" x 3½"	2¼" x 4"
Medium	D: 8 ▢	1¼"	1½"	1⅝"	1¾"	2"	2¼"
Medium 2	E: 12 ▢	1¼"	1½"	1⅝"	1¾"	2"	2¼"
Dark	F: 4 ▢	1¼"	1½"	1⅝"	1¾"	2"	2¼"

Try this: Use a different combination of mediums and darks in every block.

108

Round the Corner

5-Unit Grid

Color Illustration: page 25

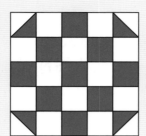
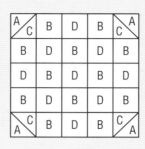
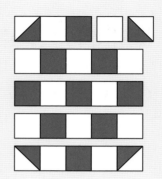

		FINISHED BLOCK SIZE					
		Single dimensions in the cutting chart indicate the size of the cut square (3" = 3" x 3").					
For 1 block:		5"	6¼"	7½"	8¾"	10"	12½"
Light	A: 2	1⅞"	2⅛"	2⅜"	2⅝"	2⅞"	3⅜"
	B: 12	1½"	1¾"	2"	2¼"	2½"	3"
Dark	C: 2	1⅞"	2⅛"	2⅜"	2⅝"	2⅞"	3⅜"
	D: 9	1½"	1¾"	2"	2¼"	2½"	3"

Try this: Use a medium instead of a dark for C.

Ruins of Jericho

8-Unit Grid

Color Illustration: page 25

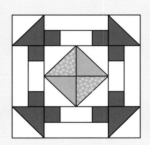
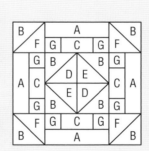
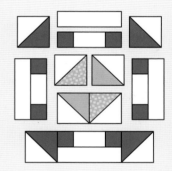

		FINISHED BLOCK SIZE					
		Single dimensions in the cutting chart indicate the size of the cut square (3" = 3" x 3").					
For 1 block:		6"	8"	9"	10"	12"	14"
Light	A: 4	1¼" x 3½"	1½" x 4½"	1⅝" x 5"	1¾" x 5½"	2" x 6½"	2¼" x 7½"
	B: 4	2⅜"	2⅞"	3⅛"	3⅜"	3⅞"	4⅜"
	C: 4	1¼" x 2"	1½" x 2½"	1⅝" x 2¾"	1¾" x 3"	2" x 3½"	2¼" x 4"
Medium	D: 1	2⅜"	2⅞"	3⅛"	3⅜"	3⅞"	4⅜"
Medium 2	E: 1	2⅜"	2⅞"	3⅛"	3⅜"	3⅞"	4⅜"
Dark	F: 2	2⅜"	2⅞"	3⅛"	3⅜"	3⅞"	4⅜"
	G: 8	1¼"	1½"	1⅝"	1¾"	2"	2¼"

Try this: Use one light for A and C and a different light for B.

□ Square(s)   ◺→◹ Square(s) cut once diagonally to make half-square triangles   ⊠→⧅ Square(s) cut twice diagonally to make quarter-square triangles   ▭ Rectangle(s)

Sawtooth II

5-Unit Grid

Color Illustration: page 26

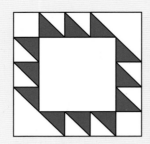 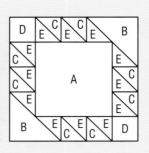 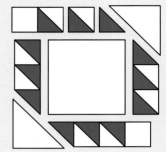

		FINISHED BLOCK SIZE					
		Single dimensions in the cutting chart indicate the size of the cut square (3" = 3" x 3").					
For 1 block:		5"	6¼"	7½"	8¾"	10"	12½"
Light	A: 1	3½"	4¼"	5"	5¾"	6½"	8"
	B: 1	2⅞"	3⅜"	3⅞"	4⅜"	4⅞"	5⅞"
	C: 4	1⅞"	2⅛"	2⅜"	2⅝"	2⅞"	3⅜"
	D: 2	1½"	1¾"	2"	2¼"	2½"	3"
Dark	E: 6	1⅞"	2⅛"	2⅜"	2⅝"	2⅞"	3⅜"

Try this: Use a large-scale print for A.

Scot's Plaid

4-Unit Grid

Color Illustration: page 26

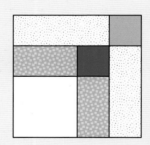 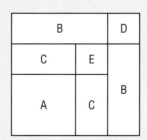 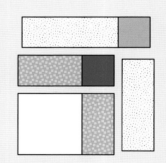

		FINISHED BLOCK SIZE					
		Single dimensions in the cutting chart indicate the size of the cut square (3" = 3" x 3").					
For 1 block:		4"	6"	8"	9"	10"	12"
Light	A: 1	2½"	3½"	4½"	5"	5½"	6½"
Light 2	B: 2	1½" x 3½"	2" x 5"	2½" x 6½"	2¾" x 7¼"	3" x 8"	3½" x 9½"
Medium	C: 2	1½" x 2½"	2" x 3½"	2½" x 4½"	2¾" x 5"	3" x 5½"	3½" x 6½"
Medium 2	D: 1	1½"	2"	2½"	2¾"	3"	3½"
Dark	E: 1	1½"	2"	2½"	2¾"	3"	3½"

Try this: Use a dark instead of medium 2 for D.

☐ Light   ⬚ Light 2   ▨ Medium   ▩ Medium 2   ■ Dark

The Sickle

4-Unit Grid

Color Illustration: page 26

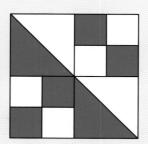 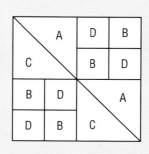 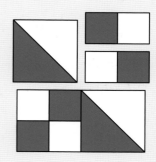

FINISHED BLOCK SIZE						
Single dimensions in the cutting chart indicate the size of the cut square (3" = 3" x 3").						
For 1 block:	**4"**	**6"**	**8"**	**9"**	**10"**	**12"**
Light A: 1 ▢→◩	2⅞"	3⅞"	4⅞"	5⅜"	5⅞"	6⅞"
B: 4 ▢	1½"	2"	2½"	2¾"	3"	3½"
Dark C: 1 ▢→◩	2⅞"	3⅞"	4⅞"	5⅜"	5⅞"	6⅞"
D: 4 ▢	1½"	2"	2½"	2¾"	3"	3½"

Try this: Use a medium instead of a light for A.

The Silent Star

3-Unit Grid

Color Illustration: page 26

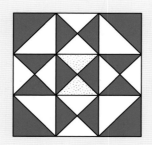 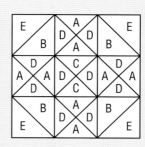 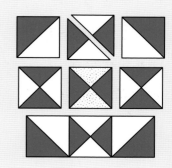

FINISHED BLOCK SIZE						
Single dimensions in the cutting chart indicate the size of the cut square (3" = 3" x 3").						
For 2 blocks:	**4½"**	**6"**	**7½"**	**9"**	**10½"**	**12"**
Light A: 4 ⊠→⧆	2¾"	3¼"	3¾"	4¼"	4¾"	5¼"
B: 4 ▢→◩	2⅜"	2⅞"	3⅜"	3⅞"	4⅜"	4⅞"
Light 2 C: 1 ⊠→⧆	2¾"	3¼"	3¾"	4¼"	4¾"	5¼"
Dark D: 5 ⊠→⧆	2¾"	3¼"	3¾"	4¼"	4¾"	5¼"
E: 4 ▢→◩	2⅜"	2⅞"	3⅜"	3⅞"	4⅜"	4⅞"

Try this: Use a medium instead of a dark for E.

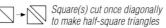 *Square(s)*   *Square(s) cut once diagonally to make half-square triangles*   ⊠→⧆ *Square(s) cut twice diagonally to make quarter-square triangles*   *Rectangle(s)*

Single Chain and Knot

10-Unit Grid

Color Illustration: page 26

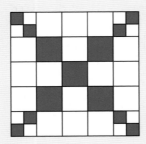

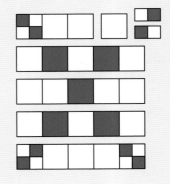

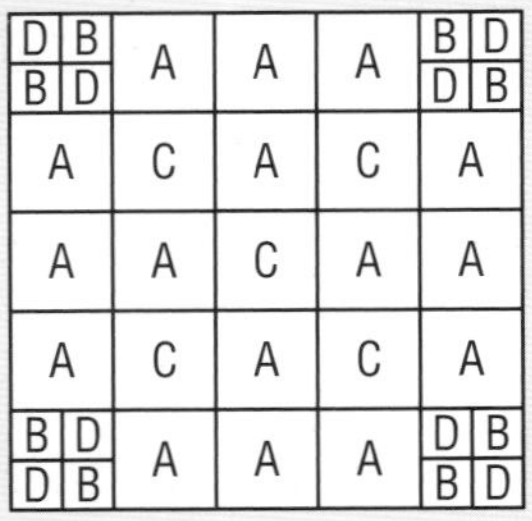

| | | | FINISHED BLOCK SIZE | | | | | |
| | | | Single dimensions in the cutting chart indicate the size of the cut square (3" = 3" x 3"). | | | | | |
For 1 block:			6¼"	7½"	8¾"	10"	12½"	13¾"
Light	A: 16		1¾"	2"	2¼"	2½"	3"	3¼"
	B: 8		1⅛"	1¼"	1⅜"	1½"	1¾"	1⅞"
Dark	C: 5		1¾"	2"	2¼"	2½"	3"	3¼"
	D: 8		1⅛"	1¼"	1⅜"	1½"	1¾"	1⅞"

Try this: Use a scrappy assortment of lights for A.

Smokehouse

6-Unit Grid

Color Illustration: page 26

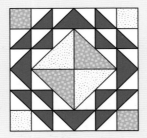
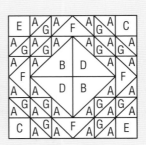

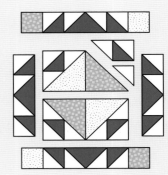

| | | | FINISHED BLOCK SIZE | | | | | |
| | | | Single dimensions in the cutting chart indicate the size of the cut square (3" = 3" x 3"). | | | | | |
For 1 block:			4½"	6"	7½"	9"	10½"	12"
Light	A: 14		1⅝"	1⅞"	2⅛"	2⅜"	2⅝"	2⅞"
Light 2	B: 1		2⅜"	2⅞"	3⅜"	3⅞"	4⅜"	4⅞"
	C: 2		1¼"	1½"	1¾"	2"	2¼"	2½"
Medium	D: 1		2⅜"	2⅞"	3⅜"	3⅞"	4⅜"	4⅞"
	E: 2		1¼"	1½"	1¾"	2"	2¼"	2½"
Dark	F: 1		2¾"	3¼"	3¾"	4¼"	4¾"	5¼"
	G: 6		1⅝"	1⅞"	2⅛"	2⅜"	2⅝"	2⅞"

Try this: Use a different light 2 and medium in every block.

Light   Light 2   Medium   Medium 2   Dark

Snowy Owl

6-Unit Grid

Color Illustration: page 26

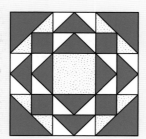 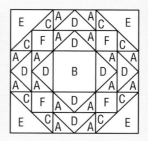 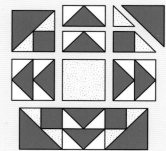

	FINISHED BLOCK SIZE					
	Single dimensions in the cutting chart indicate the size of the cut square (3" = 3" x 3").					
For 1 block:	4½"	6"	7½"	9"	10½"	12"
Light A: 8 ☐→◩	1⅝"	1⅞"	2⅛"	2⅜"	2⅝"	2⅞"
Light 2 B: 1 ☐	2"	2½"	3"	3½"	4"	4½"
C: 4 ☐→◩	1⅝"	1⅞"	2⅛"	2⅜"	2⅝"	2⅞"
Dark D: 2 ⊠→⊠	2¾"	3¼"	3¾"	4¼"	4¾"	5¼"
E: 2 ☐→◩	2⅜"	2⅞"	3⅜"	3⅞"	4⅜"	4⅞"
F: 4 ☐	1¼"	1½"	1¾"	2"	2¼"	2½"

Try this: Use a medium instead of a dark for E.

Spring and Fall

10-Unit Grid

Color Illustration: page 26

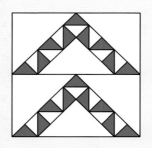 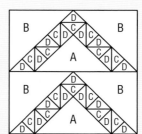 

	FINISHED BLOCK SIZE					
	Single dimensions in the cutting chart indicate the size of the cut square (3" = 3" x 3").					
For 2 blocks:	6¼"	7½"	8¾"	10"	12½"	13¾"
Light A: 1 ⊠→⊠	5"	5¾"	6½"	7¼"	8¾"	9½"
B: 4 ☐→◩	4"	4⅝"	5¼"	5⅞"	7⅛"	7¾"
C: 7 ⊠→⊠	2½"	2¾"	3"	3¼"	3¾"	4"
Dark D: 9 ⊠→⊠	2½"	2¾"	3"	3¼"	3¾"	4"

Try this: Use many different darks for D.

☐ *Square(s)*   ☐→◩ *Square(s) cut once diagonally to make half-square triangles*   ⊠→⊠ *Square(s) cut twice diagonally to make quarter-square triangles*   ☐ *Rectangle(s)*

Spruce Root Basket

6-Unit Grid

Color Illustration: page 26

FINISHED BLOCK SIZE

Single dimensions in the cutting chart indicate the size of the cut square (3" = 3" x 3").

For 1 block:		4½"	6"	7½"	9"	10½"	12"
Light	A: 12 ◻	1¼"	1½"	1¾"	2"	2¼"	2½"
Medium	B: 3 ▭	1¼" x 2"	1½" x 2½"	1¾" x 3"	2" x 3½"	2¼" x 4"	2½" x 4½"
Medium 2	C: 3 ▭	1¼" x 2"	1½" x 2½"	1¾" x 3"	2" x 3½"	2¼" x 4"	2½" x 4½"
Dark	D: 6 ▭	1¼" x 2"	1½" x 2½"	1¾" x 3"	2" x 3½"	2¼" x 4"	2½" x 4½"

Try this: Use a scrappy assortment of fabrics for B, C, and D.

Squares and Strips

11-Unit Grid

Color Illustration: page 26

FINISHED BLOCK SIZE

Single dimensions in the cutting chart indicate the size of the cut square (3" = 3" x 3").

For 1 block:		6⅞"	8¼"	9⅝"	11"	12⅜"	15⅛"
Light	A: 4 ◻	3"	3½"	4"	4½"	5"	6"
	B: 4 ▭	1⅛" x 3"	1¼" x 3½"	1⅜" x 4"	1½" x 4½"	1⅝" x 5"	1⅞" x 6"
	C: 5 ◻	1⅛"	1¼"	1⅜"	1½"	1⅝"	1⅞"
Dark	D: 8 ▭	1⅛" x 3"	1¼" x 3½"	1⅜" x 4"	1½" x 4½"	1⅝" x 5"	1⅞" x 6"
	E: 4 ◻	1⅛"	1¼"	1⅜"	1½"	1⅝"	1⅞"

Try this: Reverse the lights and darks in every other block.

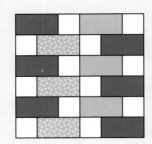

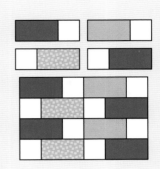

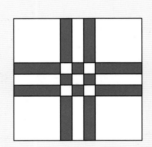

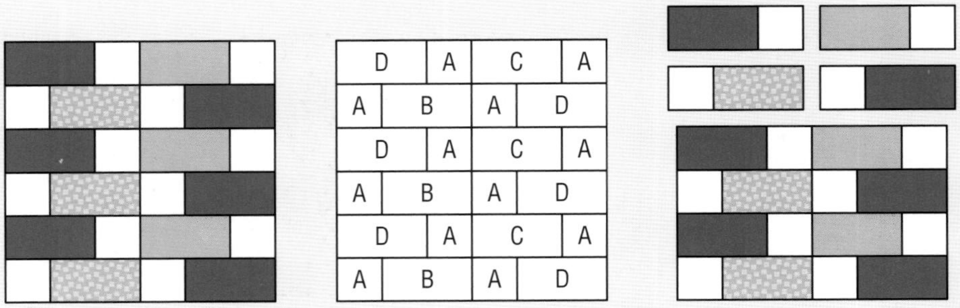

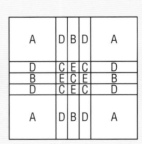

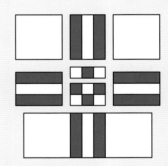

Star and Pinwheels

4-Unit Grid

Color Illustration: page 26

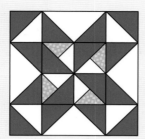
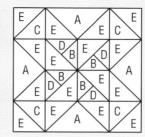
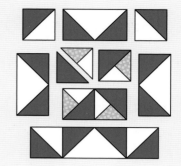

For 1 block:		FINISHED BLOCK SIZE					
		Single dimensions in the cutting chart indicate the size of the cut square (3" = 3" x 3").					
		4"	6"	8"	9"	10"	12"
Light	A: 1 ⊠→⊠	3¼"	4¼"	5¼"	5¾"	6¼"	7¼"
	B: 1 ⊠→⊠	2¼"	2¾"	3¼"	3½"	3¾"	4¼"
	C: 2 ◩→◩	1⅞"	2⅜"	2⅞"	3⅛"	3⅜"	3⅞"
Medium	D: 1 ⊠→⊠	2¼"	2¾"	3¼"	3½"	3¾"	4¼"
Dark	E: 8 ◩→◩	1⅞"	2⅜"	2⅞"	3⅛"	3⅜"	3⅞"

Try this: Reverse the lights and mediums in every other block.

Star Puzzle

4-Unit Grid

Color Illustration: page 26

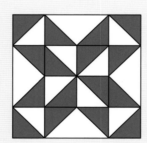
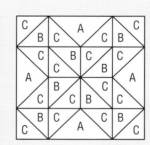
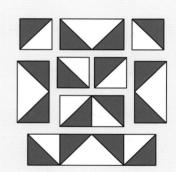

For 1 block:		FINISHED BLOCK SIZE					
		Single dimensions in the cutting chart indicate the size of the cut square (3" = 3" x 3").					
		4"	6"	8"	9"	10"	12"
Light	A: 1 ⊠→⊠	3¼"	4¼"	5¼"	5¾"	6¼"	7¼"
	B: 4 ◩→◩	1⅞"	2⅜"	2⅞"	3⅛"	3⅜"	3⅞"
Dark	C: 8 ◩→◩	1⅞"	2⅜"	2⅞"	3⅛"	3⅜"	3⅞"

Try this: Use a medium instead of a light for A and B.

☐ *Square(s)*   ◩→◩ *Square(s) cut once diagonally to make half-square triangles*   ⊠→⊠ *Square(s) cut twice diagonally to make quarter-square triangles*   ▭ *Rectangle(s)*

State of Georgia

5-Unit Grid

Color Illustration: page 27

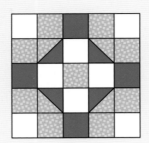
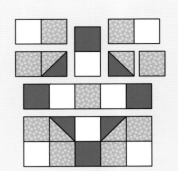

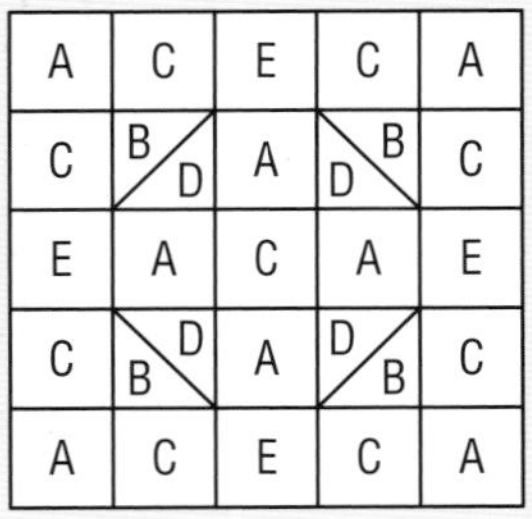

For 1 block:		FINISHED BLOCK SIZE					
		Single dimensions in the cutting chart indicate the size of the cut square (3" = 3" x 3").					
		5"	6¼"	7½"	8¾"	10"	12½"
Light	A: 8 □	1½"	1¾"	2"	2¼"	2½"	3"
Medium	B: 2 ◨→◪	1⅞"	2⅛"	2⅜"	2⅝"	2⅞"	3⅜"
	C: 9 □	1½"	1¾"	2"	2¼"	2½"	3"
Dark	D: 2 ◨→◪	1⅞"	2⅛"	2⅜"	2⅝"	2⅞"	3⅜"
	E: 4 □	1½"	1¾"	2"	2¼"	2½"	3"

Try this: Use a light instead of a medium for B.

Stepping Stones

6-Unit Grid

Color Illustration: page 27

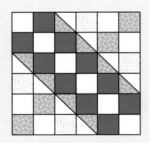
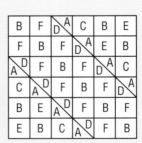
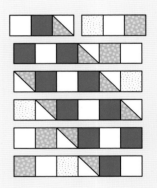

For 1 block:		FINISHED BLOCK SIZE					
		Single dimensions in the cutting chart indicate the size of the cut square (3" = 3" x 3").					
		4½"	6"	7½"	9"	10½"	12"
Light	A: 4 ◨→◪	1⅝"	1⅞"	2⅛"	2⅜"	2⅝"	2⅞"
	B: 10 □	1¼"	1½"	1¾"	2"	2¼"	2½"
Light 2	C: 4 □	1¼"	1½"	1¾"	2"	2¼"	2½"
Medium	D: 4 ◨→◪	1⅝"	1⅞"	2⅛"	2⅜"	2⅝"	2⅞"
	E: 4 □	1¼"	1½"	1¾"	2"	2¼"	2½"
Dark	F: 10 □	1¼"	1½"	1¾"	2"	2¼"	2½"

Try this: Use a scrappy assortment of light fabrics for C and a scrappy assortment of medium fabrics for E.

□ Light ▫ Light 2 ▨ Medium ▩ Medium 2 ■ Dark

Stiles and Paths

9-Unit Grid

Color Illustration: page 27

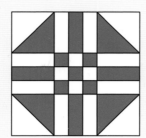 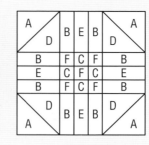 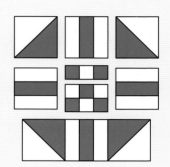

For 1 block:		FINISHED BLOCK SIZE Single dimensions in the cutting chart indicate the size of the cut square (3" = 3" x 3").					
		6¾"	9"	10⅛"	11¼"	12⅜"	13½"
Light	A: 2 ▧→◪	3⅛"	3⅞"	4¼"	4⅝"	5"	5⅜"
	B: 8 ▭	1¼" x 2¾"	1½" x 3½"	1⅝" x 3⅞"	1¾" x 4¼"	1⅞" x 4⅝"	2" x 5"
	C: 4 ☐	1¼"	1½"	1⅝"	1¾"	1⅞"	2"
Dark	D: 2 ▧→◪	3⅛"	3⅞"	4¼"	4⅝"	5"	5⅜"
	E: 4 ▭	1¼" x 2¾"	1½" x 3½"	1⅝" x 3⅞"	1¾" x 4¼"	1⅞" x 4⅝"	2" x 5"
	F: 5 ☐	1¼"	1½"	1⅝"	1¾"	1⅞"	2"

Try this: Use a medium instead of a dark in every other block.

Stockyard's Star for Nebraska

8-Unit Grid

Color Illustration: page 27

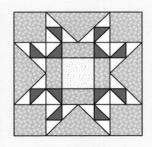 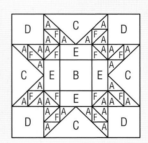 

For 1 block:		FINISHED BLOCK SIZE Single dimensions in the cutting chart indicate the size of the cut square (3" = 3" x 3").					
		6"	8"	9"	10"	12"	14"
Light	A: 14 ▧→◪	1⅝"	1⅞"	2"	2⅛"	2⅜"	2⅝"
Light 2	B: 1 ☐	2"	2½"	2¾"	3"	3½"	4"
Medium	C: 1 ⊠→⊠	4¼"	5¼"	5¾"	6¼"	7¼"	8¼"
	D: 4 ☐	2"	2½"	2¾"	3"	3½"	4"
	E: 4 ▭	1¼" x 2"	1½" x 2½"	1⅝" x 2¾"	1¾" x 3"	2" x 3½"	2¼" x 4"
Dark	F: 6 ▧→◪	1⅝"	1⅞"	2"	2⅛"	2⅜"	2⅝"

Try this: Use the same medium for C and D and a different medium for E.

☐ Square(s)   ▧→◪ Square(s) cut once diagonally to make half-square triangles   ⊠→⊠ Square(s) cut twice diagonally to make quarter-square triangles   ▭ Rectangle(s)

Strip Heart

8-Unit Grid

Color Illustration: page 27

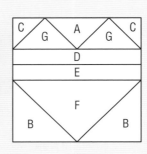
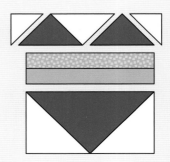

	FINISHED BLOCK SIZE					
	Single dimensions in the cutting chart indicate the size of the cut square (3" = 3" x 3").					

For 4 blocks:		6"	8"	9"	10"	12"	14"
Light	A: 1 ⊠→⊠	4¼"	5¼"	5¾"	6¼"	7¼"	8¼"
	B: 4 ◺→◺	3⅞"	4⅞"	5⅜"	5⅞"	6⅞"	7⅞"
	C: 4 ◺→◺	2⅜"	2⅞"	3⅛"	3⅜"	3⅞"	4⅜"
Medium	D: 4 ▭	1¼" x 6½"	1½" x 8½"	1⅝" x 9½"	1¾" x 10½"	2" x 12½"	2¼" x 14½"
Medium 2	E: 4 ▭	1¼" x 6½"	1½" x 8½"	1⅝" x 9½"	1¾" x 10½"	2" x 12½"	2¼" x 14½"
Dark	F: 1 ⊠→⊠	7¼"	9¼"	10¼"	11¼"	13¼"	15¼"
	G: 2 ⊠→⊠	4¼"	5¼"	5¾"	6¼"	7¼"	8¼"

Try this: Use a different combination of mediums in every block.

Summer Solstice

4-Unit Grid

Color Illustration: page 27

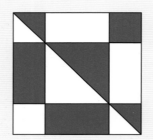
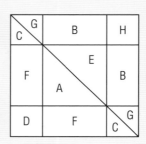
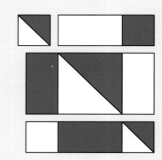

	FINISHED BLOCK SIZE					
	Single dimensions in the cutting chart indicate the size of the cut square (3" = 3" x 3").					

For 2 blocks:		4"	6"	8"	9"	10"	12"
Light	A: 1 ◺→◺	2⅞"	3⅞"	4⅞"	5⅜"	5⅞"	6⅞"
	B: 4 ▭	1½" x 2½"	2" x 3½"	2½" x 4½"	2¾" x 5"	3" x 5½"	3½" x 6½"
	C: 2 ◺→◺	1⅞"	2⅜"	2⅞"	3⅛"	3⅜"	3⅞"
	D: 2 ▢	1½"	2"	2½"	2¾"	3"	3½"
Dark	E: 1 ◺→◺	2⅞"	3⅞"	4⅞"	5⅜"	5⅞"	6⅞"
	F: 4 ▭	1½" x 2½"	2" x 3½"	2½" x 4½"	2¾" x 5"	3" x 5½"	3½" x 6½"
	G: 2 ◺→◺	1⅞"	2⅜"	2⅞"	3⅛"	3⅜"	3⅞"
	H: 2 ▢	1½"	2"	2½"	2¾"	3"	3½"

Try this: Use a medium instead of a light in every other block.

▢ Light	▦ Light 2	▨ Medium	▥ Medium 2	■ Dark

Surprise Package

7-Unit Grid

Color Illustration: page 27

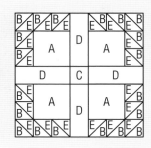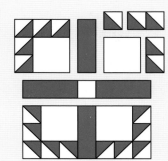

		FINISHED BLOCK SIZE					
		Single dimensions in the cutting chart indicate the size of the cut square (3" = 3" x 3").					
For 1 block:		5¼"	7"	8¾"	10½"	12¼"	14"
Light	A: 4 ☐	2"	2½"	3"	3½"	4"	4½"
	B: 10 ◨→◺	1⅝"	1⅞"	2⅛"	2⅜"	2⅝"	2⅞"
	C: 1 ☐	1¼"	1½"	1¾"	2"	2¼"	2½"
Dark	D: 4 ▭	1¼" x 2¾"	1½" x 3½"	1¾" x 4¼"	2" x 5"	2¼" x 5¾"	2½" x 6½"
	E: 10 ◨→◺	1⅝"	1⅞"	2⅛"	2⅜"	2⅝"	2⅞"

Try this: Use a medium instead of a dark for D.

Tea Rose

7-Unit Grid

Color Illustration: page 27

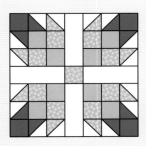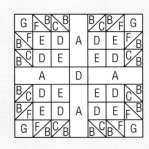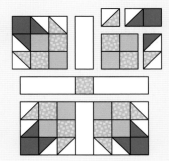

		FINISHED BLOCK SIZE					
		Single dimensions in the cutting chart indicate the size of the cut square (3" = 3" x 3").					
For 1 block:		5¼"	7"	8¾"	10½"	12¼"	14"
Light	A: 4 ▭	1¼" x 2¾"	1½" x 3½"	1¾" x 4¼"	2" x 5"	2¼" x 5¾"	2½" x 6½"
	B: 8 ◨→◺	1⅝"	1⅞"	2⅛"	2⅜"	2⅝"	2⅞"
Medium	C: 4 ◨→◺	1⅝"	1⅞"	2⅛"	2⅜"	2⅝"	2⅞"
	D: 9 ☐	1¼"	1½"	1¾"	2"	2¼"	2½"
Medium 2	E: 8 ☐	1¼"	1½"	1¾"	2"	2¼"	2½"
Dark	F: 4 ◨→◺	1⅝"	1⅞"	2⅛"	2⅜"	2⅝"	2⅞"
	G: 4 ☐	1¼"	1½"	1¾"	2"	2¼"	2½"

Try this: Use a dark instead of a medium for D.

Square(s) Square(s) cut once diagonally to make half-square triangles Square(s) cut twice diagonally to make quarter-square triangles Rectangle(s)

119

Texas Puzzle

9-Unit Grid

Color Illustration: page 27

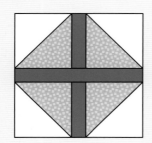 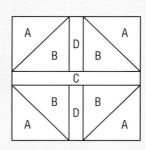 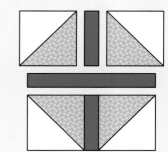

		FINISHED BLOCK SIZE					
		Single dimensions in the cutting chart indicate the size of the cut square (3" = 3" x 3").					
For 1 block:		6¾"	9"	10⅛"	11¼"	12⅜"	13½"
Light	A: 2	3⅞"	4⅞"	5⅜"	5⅞"	6⅜"	6⅞"
Medium	B: 2	3⅞"	4⅞"	5⅜"	5⅞"	6⅜"	6⅞"
Dark	C: 1	1¼" x 7¼"	1½" x 9½"	1⅝" x 10⅝"	1¾" x 11¾"	1⅞" x 12⅞"	2" x 14"
	D: 2	1¼" x 3½"	1½" x 4½"	1⅝" x 5"	1¾" x 5½"	1⅞" x 6"	2" x 6½"

Try this: Use a different combination of mediums and lights in every block.

Three and Six

3-Unit Grid

Color Illustration: page 27

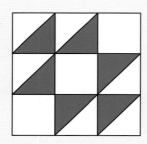 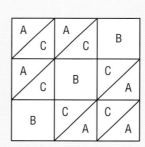 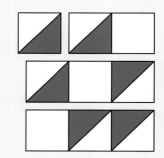

		FINISHED BLOCK SIZE					
		Single dimensions in the cutting chart indicate the size of the cut square (3" = 3" x 3").					
For 1 block:		4½"	6"	7½"	9"	10½"	12"
Light	A: 3	2⅜"	2⅞"	3⅜"	3⅞"	4⅜"	4⅞"
	B: 3	2"	2½"	3"	3½"	4"	4½"
Dark	C: 3	2⅜"	2⅞"	3⅜"	3⅞"	4⅜"	4⅞"

Try this: Use a different dark in every block.

Light   Light 2   Medium   Medium 2   Dark

Tonganoxie Nine Patch

7-Unit Grid

Color Illustration: page 27

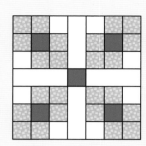

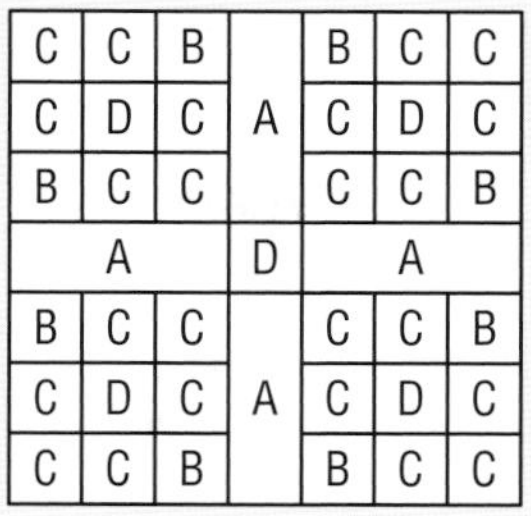

C	C	B		B	C	C
C	D	C	A	C	D	C
B	C	C		C	C	B
			A		D		A		
B	C	C		C	C	B
C	D	C	A	C	D	C
C	C	B		B	C	C

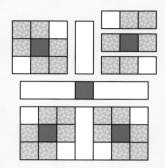

FINISHED BLOCK SIZE						
Single dimensions in the cutting chart indicate the size of the cut square (3" = 3" x 3").						
For 1 block:		5¼"	7"	8¾"	10½"	12¼"	14"

For 1 block:		5¼"	7"	8¾"	10½"	12¼"	14"
Light	A: 4	1¼" x 2¾"	1½" x 3½"	1¾" x 4¼"	2" x 5"	2¼" x 5¾"	2½" x 6½"
	B: 8	1¼"	1½"	1¾"	2"	2¼"	2½"
Medium	C: 24	1¼"	1½"	1¾"	2"	2¼"	2½"
Dark	D: 5	1¼"	1½"	1¾"	2"	2¼"	2½"

Try this: Use several different mediums for C.

Trail of Tears

4-Unit Grid

Color Illustration: page 27

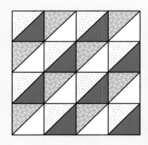

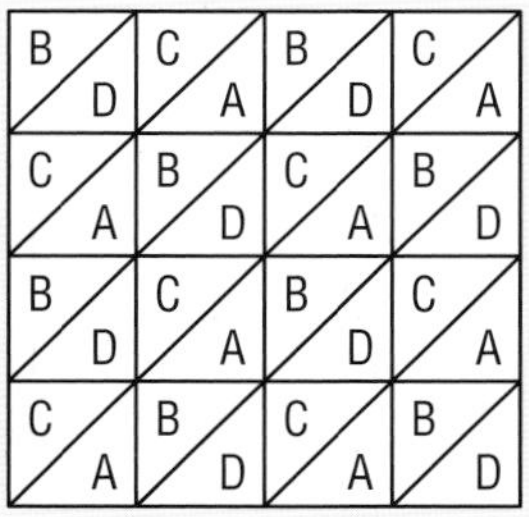

B	C	B	C
D	A	D	A
C	B	C	B
A	D	A	D
B	C	B	C
D	A	D	A
C	B	C	B
A	D	A	D

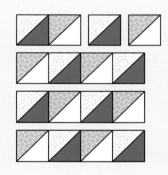

FINISHED BLOCK SIZE						
Single dimensions in the cutting chart indicate the size of the cut square (3" = 3" x 3").						

For 1 block:		4"	6"	8"	9"	10"	12"
Light	A: 4	1⅞"	2⅜"	2⅞"	3⅛"	3⅜"	3⅞"
Light 2	B: 4	1⅞"	2⅜"	2⅞"	3⅛"	3⅜"	3⅞"
Medium	C: 4	1⅞"	2⅜"	2⅞"	3⅛"	3⅜"	3⅞"
Dark	D: 4	1⅞"	2⅜"	2⅞"	3⅛"	3⅜"	3⅞"

Try this: Use a scrappy assortment of fabrics for B, C, and D.

Square(s) Square(s) cut once diagonally to make half-square triangles Square(s) cut twice diagonally to make quarter-square triangles Rectangle(s)

Triangle

6-Unit Grid

Color Illustration: page 28

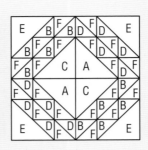
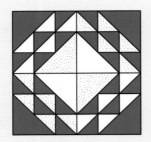
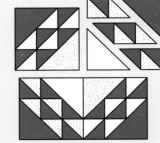

			FINISHED BLOCK SIZE				
			Single dimensions in the cutting chart indicate the size of the cut square (3" = 3" x 3").				
For 1 block:			4½"	6"	7½"	9"	10½"	12"
Light	A: 1		2⅜"	2⅞"	3⅜"	3⅞"	4⅜"	4⅞"
	B: 5		1⅝"	1⅞"	2⅛"	2⅜"	2⅝"	2⅞"
Light 2	C: 1		2⅜"	2⅞"	3⅜"	3⅞"	4⅜"	4⅞"
	D: 5		1⅝"	1⅞"	2⅛"	2⅜"	2⅝"	2⅞"
Dark	E: 2		2⅜"	2⅞"	3⅜"	3⅞"	4⅜"	4⅞"
	F: 10		1⅝"	1⅞"	2⅛"	2⅜"	2⅝"	2⅞"

Try this: Use a different combination of fabrics in each quadrant of the block.

Triplet

3-Unit Grid

Color Illustration: page 28

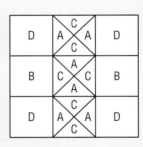
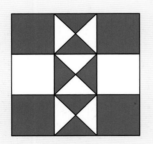
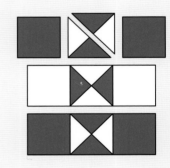

			FINISHED BLOCK SIZE				
			Single dimensions in the cutting chart indicate the size of the cut square (3" = 3" x 3").				
For 2 blocks:			4½"	6"	7½"	9"	10½"	12"
Light	A: 3		2¾"	3¼"	3¾"	4¼"	4¾"	5¼"
	B: 4		2"	2½"	3"	3½"	4"	4½"
Dark	C: 3		2¾"	3¼"	3¾"	4¼"	4¾"	5¼"
	D: 8		2"	2½"	3"	3½"	4"	4½"

Try this: Reverse the lights and darks in every other block.

Light   Light 2   Medium   Medium 2   Dark

Twelve Crowns

12-Unit Grid

Color Illustration: page 28

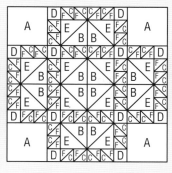
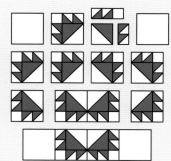

		FINISHED BLOCK SIZE					
		Single dimensions in the cutting chart indicate the size of the cut square (3" = 3" x 3").					
For 1 block:		6"	7½"	9"	12"	13½"	15"
Light	A: 4 ☐	2"	2⅜"	2¾"	3½"	3⅞"	4¼"
	B: 6 ◹→◺	1⅞"	2⅛"	2⅜"	2⅞"	3⅛"	3⅜"
	C: 24 ◹→◺	1⅜"	1½"	1⅝"	1⅞"	2"	2⅛"
	D: 12 ☐	1"	1⅛"	1¼"	1½"	1⅝"	1¾"
Dark	E: 6 ◹→◺	1⅞"	2⅛"	2⅜"	2⅞"	3⅛"	3⅜"
	F: 24 ◹→◺	1⅜"	1½"	1⅝"	1⅞"	2"	2⅛"

Try this: Use a different fabric combination for each "crown."

Vermont

4-Unit Grid

Color Illustration: page 28

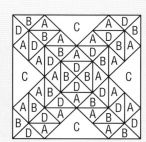

		FINISHED BLOCK SIZE					
		Single dimensions in the cutting chart indicate the size of the cut square (3" = 3" x 3").					
For 2 blocks:		4"	6"	8"	9"	10"	12"
Light	A: 10 ⊠→⧅	2¼"	2¾"	3¼"	3½"	3¾"	4¼"
Medium	B: 7 ⊠→⧅	2¼"	2¾"	3¼"	3½"	3¾"	4¼"
Dark	C: 2 ⊠→⧅	3¼"	4¼"	5¼"	5¾"	6¼"	7¼"
	D: 7 ⊠→⧅	2¼"	2¾"	3¼"	3½"	3¾"	4¼"

Try this: Use one dark for C and a different dark for D.

☐ *Square(s)*	◹→◺ *Square(s) cut once diagonally to make half-square triangles*	⊠→⧅ *Square(s) cut twice diagonally to make quarter-square triangles*	▭ *Rectangle(s)*

Vice President's Block

5-Unit Grid

Color Illustration: page 28

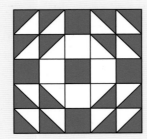
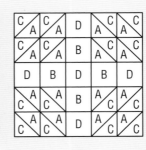
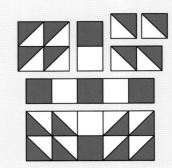

Note: *This block is identical to Judy's Choice (page 82) in size, shape, and position of the pieces, but the value arrangement is different.*

		FINISHED BLOCK SIZE					
		Single dimensions in the cutting chart indicate the size of the cut square (3" = 3" x 3")					
For 1 block:		5"	6¼"	7½"	8¾"	10"	12½"
Light	A: 8 ☐→◪	1⅞"	2⅛"	2⅜"	2⅝"	2⅞"	3⅜"
	B: 4 ☐	1½"	1¾"	2"	2¼"	2½"	3"
Dark	C: 8 ☐→◪	1⅞"	2⅛"	2⅜"	2⅝"	2⅞"	3⅜"
	D: 5 ☐	1½"	1¾"	2"	2¼"	2½"	3"

Try this: Use a different combination of lights and darks in every block.

Vines at the Window

8-Unit Grid

Color Illustration: page 28

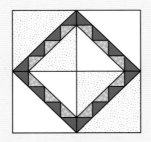
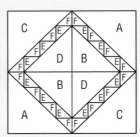

		FINISHED BLOCK SIZE					
		Single dimensions in the cutting chart indicate the size of the cut square (3" = 3" x 3").					
For 1 block:		6"	8"	9"	10"	12"	14"
Light	A: 1 ☐→◪	3⅞"	4⅞"	5⅜"	5⅞"	6⅞"	7⅞"
	B: 1 ☐→◪	3⅛"	3⅞"	4¼"	4⅝"	5⅜"	6⅛"
Light 2	C: 1 ☐→◪	3⅞"	4⅞"	5⅜"	5⅞"	6⅞"	7⅞"
	D: 1 ☐→◪	3⅛"	3⅞"	4¼"	4⅝"	5⅜"	6⅛"
Medium	E: 6 ☐→◪	1⅝"	1⅞"	2"	2⅛"	2⅜"	2⅝"
Dark	F: 8 ☐→◪	1⅝"	1⅞"	2"	2⅛"	2⅜"	2⅝"

Try this: Use several different mediums for E.

☐ Light ░ Light 2 ▤ Medium ▥ Medium 2 ■ Dark

Wagon Tracks

6-Unit Grid

Color Illustration: page 28

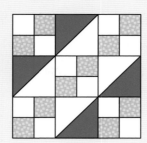
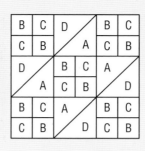
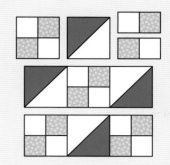

		FINISHED BLOCK SIZE					
		Single dimensions in the cutting chart indicate the size of the cut square (3" = 3" x 3").					
For 1 block:		4½"	6"	7½"	9"	10½"	12"
Light	A: 2 ◻→◺	2⅜"	2⅞"	3⅜"	3⅞"	4⅜"	4⅞"
	B: 10 ◻	1¼"	1½"	1¾"	2"	2¼"	2½"
Medium	C: 10 ◻	1¼"	1½"	1¾"	2"	2¼"	2½"
Dark	D: 2 ◻→◺	2⅜"	2⅞"	3⅜"	3⅞"	4⅜"	4⅞"

Try this: Use one light for A and a different light for B.

Washington Star

8-Unit Grid

Color Illustration: page 28

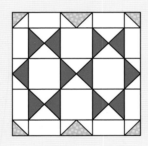
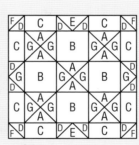
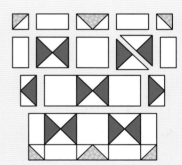

		FINISHED BLOCK SIZE					
		Single dimensions in the cutting chart indicate the size of the cut square (3" = 3" x 3").					
For 2 blocks:		6"	8"	9"	10"	12"	14"
Light	A: 5 ⊠→⧆	2¾"	3¼"	3½"	3¾"	4¼"	4¾"
	B: 8 ◻	2"	2½"	2¾"	3"	3½"	4"
	C: 16 ▭	1¼" x 2"	1½" x 2½"	1⅝" x 2¾"	1¾" x 3"	2" x 3½"	2¼" x 4"
	D: 12 ◻→◺	1⅝"	1⅞"	2"	2⅛"	2⅜"	2⅝"
Medium	E: 1 ⊠→⧆	2¾"	3¼"	3½"	3¾"	4¼"	4¾"
	F: 4 ◻→◺	1⅝"	1⅞"	2"	2⅛"	2⅜"	2⅝"
Dark	G: 6 ⊠→⧆	2¾"	3¼"	3½"	3¾"	4¼"	4¾"

Try this: Use a different dark for each elongated star.

◻ Square(s)	◻→◺ Square(s) cut once diagonally to make half-square triangles	⊠→⧆ Square(s) cut twice diagonally to make quarter-square triangles	▭ Rectangle(s)

Water Wheel

6-Unit Grid

Color Illustration: page 28

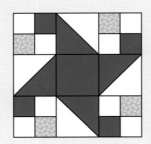
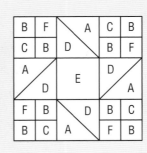
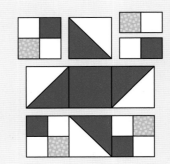

		FINISHED BLOCK SIZE					
		Single dimensions in the cutting chart indicate the size of the cut square (3" = 3" x 3").					
For 1 block:		4½"	6"	7½"	9"	10½"	12"
Light	A: 2	2⅜"	2⅞"	3⅜"	3⅞"	4⅜"	4⅞"
	B: 8	1¼"	1½"	1¾"	2"	2¼"	2½"
Medium	C: 4	1¼"	1½"	1¾"	2"	2¼"	2½"
Dark	D: 2	2⅜"	2⅞"	3⅜"	3⅞"	4⅜"	4⅞"
	E: 1	2"	2½"	3"	3½"	4"	4½"
	F: 4	1¼"	1½"	1¾"	2"	2¼"	2½"

Try this: Use a different medium in each block.

Whales' Tails

8-Unit Grid

Color Illustration: page 28

Note: *This block is identical to Wild Geese (page 128) in size, shape, and position of the pieces, but the value arrangement is different.*

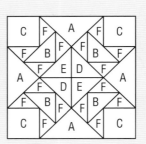

		FINISHED BLOCK SIZE					
		Single dimensions in the cutting chart indicate the size of the cut square (3" = 3" x 3").					
For 1 block:		6"	8"	9"	10"	12"	14"
Light	A: 1	4¼"	5¼"	5¾"	6¼"	7¼"	8¼"
	B: 2	2⅜"	2⅞"	3⅛"	3⅜"	3⅞"	4⅜"
	C: 4	2"	2½"	2¾"	3"	3½"	4"
Medium	D: 1	2⅜"	2⅞"	3⅛"	3⅜"	3⅞"	4⅜"
Medium 2	E: 1	2⅜"	2⅞"	3⅛"	3⅜"	3⅞"	4⅜"
Dark	F: 4	2¾"	3¼"	3½"	3¾"	4¼"	4¾"

Try this: Use the same light for A and C and a different light for B.

	Light		Light 2		Medium		Medium 2		Dark

Wheel of Chance

5-Unit Grid

Color Illustration: page 28

Note: *This block is identical to Alpine Cross (page 32) in size, shape, and position of the pieces, but the value arrangement is different.*

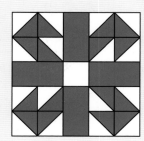 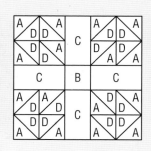 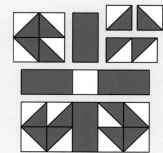

FINISHED BLOCK SIZE						
Single dimensions in the cutting chart indicate the size of the cut square (3" = 3" x 3").						
For 1 block:	5"	6¼"	7½"	8¾"	10"	12½"
Light A: 8	1⅞"	2⅛"	2⅜"	2⅝"	2⅞"	3⅜"
B: 1	1½"	1¾"	2"	2¼"	2½"	3"
Dark C: 4	1½" x 2½"	1¾" x 3"	2" x 3½"	2¼" x 4"	2½" x 4½"	3" x 5½"
D: 8	1⅞"	2⅛"	2⅜"	2⅝"	2⅞"	3⅜"

Try this: Use one medium for C and several different darks for D.

Whirling Square

9-Unit Grid

Color Illustration: page 28

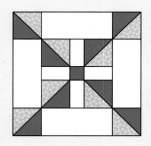 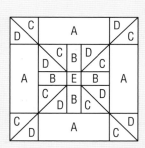 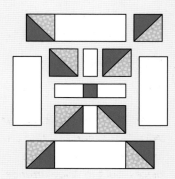

FINISHED BLOCK SIZE						
Single dimensions in the cutting chart indicate the size of the cut square (3" = 3" x 3").						
For 1 block:	6¾"	9"	10⅛"	11¼"	12⅜"	13½"
Light A: 4	2" x 4¼"	2½" x 5½"	2¾" x 6⅛"	3" x 6¾"	3¼" x 7⅜"	3½" x 8"
B: 4	1¼" x 2"	1½" x 2½"	1⅝" x 2¾"	1¾" x 3"	1⅞" x 3¼"	2" x 3½"
Medium C: 4	2⅜"	2⅞"	3⅛"	3⅜"	3⅝"	3⅞"
Dark D: 4	2⅜"	2⅞"	3⅛"	3⅜"	3⅝"	3⅞"
E: 1	1¼"	1½"	1⅝"	1¾"	1⅞"	2"

Try this: Use a scrappy assortment of mediums and darks for C and D.

☐ Square(s)	◹→◨ Square(s) cut once diagonally to make half-square triangles	⊠→⧅ Square(s) cut twice diagonally to make quarter-square triangles	▭ Rectangle(s)

Wild Duck

4-Unit Grid

Color Illustration: page 29

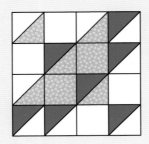
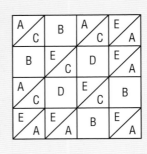
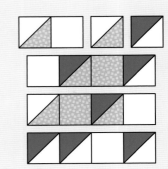

		FINISHED BLOCK SIZE					
		Single dimensions in the cutting chart indicate the size of the cut square (3" = 3" x 3").					
For 2 blocks:		4"	6"	8"	9"	10"	12"
Light	A: 8 ⬜→◨	1⅞"	2⅜"	2⅞"	3⅛"	3⅜"	3⅞"
	B: 8 ⬜	1½"	2"	2½"	2¾"	3"	3½"
Medium	C: 5 ⬜→◨	1⅞"	2⅜"	2⅞"	3⅛"	3⅜"	3⅞"
	D: 4 ⬜	1½"	2"	2½"	2¾"	3"	3½"
Dark	E: 7 ⬜→◨	1⅞"	2⅜"	2⅞"	3⅛"	3⅜"	3⅞"

Try this: Use a different combination of mediums and darks in every block.

Wild Geese

8-Unit Grid

Color Illustration: page 29

Note: This block is identical to Whales' Tails (page 126) in size, shape, and position of the pieces, but the value arrangement is different.

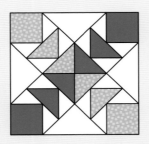
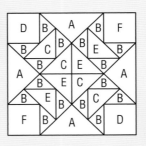
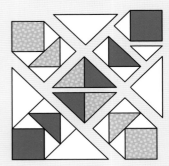

		FINISHED BLOCK SIZE					
		Single dimensions in the cutting chart indicate the size of the cut square (3" = 3" x 3").					
For 1 block:		6"	8"	9"	10"	12"	14"
Light	A: 1 ⊠→⊠	4¼"	5¼"	5¾"	6¼"	7¼"	8¼"
	B: 4 ⊠→⊠	2¾"	3¼"	3½"	3¾"	4¼"	4¾"
Medium	C: 2 ⬜→◨	2⅜"	2⅞"	3⅛"	3⅜"	3⅞"	4⅜"
	D: 2 ⬜	2"	2½"	2¾"	3"	3½"	4"
Dark	E: 2 ⬜→◨	2⅜"	2⅞"	3⅛"	3⅜"	3⅞"	4⅜"
	F: 2 ⬜	2"	2½"	2¾"	3"	3½"	4"

Try this: Use a different light in every block.

⬜ Light   ▦ Light 2   ▦ Medium   ⬛ Medium 2   ⬛ Dark

Wild Goose Chase IV

5-Unit Grid

Color Illustration: page 29

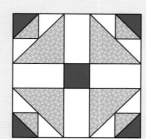
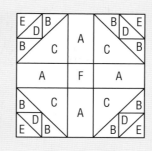
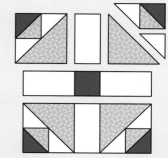

FINISHED BLOCK SIZE

Single dimensions in the cutting chart indicate the size of the cut square (3" = 3" x 3").

For 1 block:		5"	6¼"	7½"	8¾"	10"	12½"
Light	A: 4 ▢	1½" x 2½"	1¾" x 3"	2" x 3½"	2¼" x 4"	2½" x 4½"	3" x 5½"
	B: 4 ◨→◩	1⅞"	2⅛"	2⅜"	2⅝"	2⅞"	3⅜"
Medium	C: 2 ◨→◩	2⅞"	3⅜"	3⅞"	4⅜"	4⅞"	5⅞"
	D: 2 ◨→◩	1⅞"	2⅛"	2⅜"	2⅝"	2⅞"	3⅜"
Dark	E: 2 ◨→◩	1⅞"	2⅛"	2⅜"	2⅝"	2⅞"	3⅜"
	F: 1 ▢	1½"	1¾"	2"	2¼"	2½"	3"

Try this: Reverse the mediums and darks in every other block.

Windmill II

4-Unit Grid

Color Illustration: page 29

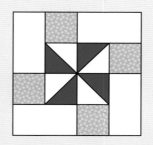
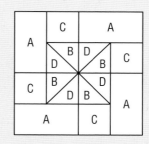
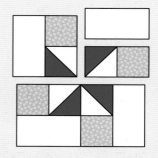

FINISHED BLOCK SIZE

Single dimensions in the cutting chart indicate the size of the cut square (3" = 3" x 3").

For 1 block:		4"	6"	8"	9"	10"	12"
Light	A: 4 ▢	1½" x 2½"	2" x 3½"	2½" x 4½"	2¾" x 5"	3" x 5½"	3½" x 6½"
	B: 2 ◨→◩	1⅞"	2⅜"	2⅞"	3⅛"	3⅜"	3⅞"
Medium	C: 4 ▢	1½"	2"	2½"	2¾"	3"	3½"
Dark	D: 2 ◨→◩	1⅞"	2⅜"	2⅞"	3⅛"	3⅜"	3⅞"

Try this: Use several different mediums for C.

Windmill III

8-Unit Grid

Color Illustration: page 29

 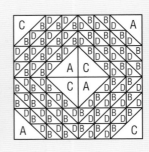 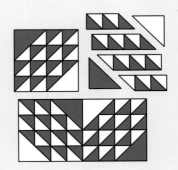

		FINISHED BLOCK SIZE					
		Single dimensions in the cutting chart indicate the size of the cut square (3" = 3" x 3").					
For 1 block:		6"	8"	9"	10"	12"	14"
Light	A: 2	2³⁄₈"	2⁷⁄₈"	3¹⁄₈"	3³⁄₈"	3⁷⁄₈"	4³⁄₈"
	B: 24	1⁵⁄₈"	1⁷⁄₈"	2"	2¹⁄₈"	2³⁄₈"	2⁵⁄₈"
Dark	C: 2	2³⁄₈"	2⁷⁄₈"	3¹⁄₈"	3³⁄₈"	3⁷⁄₈"	4³⁄₈"
	D: 24	1⁵⁄₈"	1⁷⁄₈"	2"	2¹⁄₈"	2³⁄₈"	2⁵⁄₈"

Try this: Use many different darks for D.

The Winged 9 Patch

8-Unit Grid

Color Illustration: page 29

 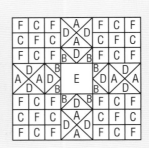 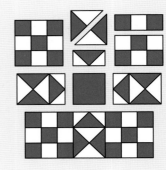

		FINISHED BLOCK SIZE					
		Single dimensions in the cutting chart indicate the size of the cut square (3" = 3" x 3").					
For 1 block:		6"	8"	9"	10"	12"	14"
Light	A: 2	2³⁄₄"	3¹⁄₄"	3¹⁄₂"	3³⁄₄"	4¹⁄₄"	4³⁄₄"
	B: 4	1⁵⁄₈"	1⁷⁄₈"	2"	2¹⁄₈"	2³⁄₈"	2⁵⁄₈"
	C: 16	1¹⁄₄"	1¹⁄₂"	1⁵⁄₈"	1³⁄₄"	2"	2¹⁄₄"
Dark	D: 3	2³⁄₄"	3¹⁄₄"	3¹⁄₂"	3³⁄₄"	4¹⁄₄"	4³⁄₄"
	E: 1	2"	2¹⁄₂"	2³⁄₄"	3"	3¹⁄₂"	4"
	F: 20	1¹⁄₄"	1¹⁄₂"	1⁵⁄₈"	1³⁄₄"	2"	2¹⁄₄"

Try this: Use a medium instead of a dark for F.

☐ Light   ▦ Light 2   ▨ Medium   ▨ Medium 2   ■ Dark

Winged Square

6-Unit Grid

Color Illustration: page 29

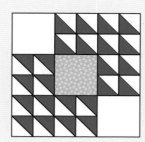 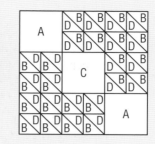 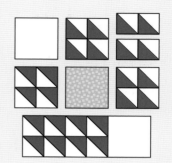

				FINISHED BLOCK SIZE				
				Single dimensions in the cutting chart indicate the size of the cut square (3" = 3" x 3").				
For 1 block:			4½"	6"	7½"	9"	10½"	12"
Light	A: 2		2"	2½"	3"	3½"	4"	4½"
	B: 12		1⅝"	1⅞"	2⅛"	2⅜"	2⅝"	2⅞"
Medium	C: 1		2"	2½"	3"	3½"	4"	4½"
Dark	D: 12		1⅝"	1⅞"	2⅛"	2⅜"	2⅝"	2⅞"

Try this: Use a different combination of mediums and darks in every block.

Wishing Ring

5-Unit Grid

Color Illustration: page 29

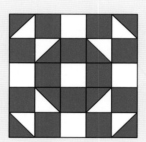 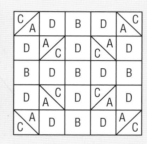 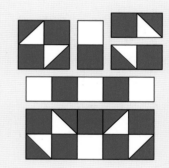

			FINISHED BLOCK SIZE					
			Single dimensions in the cutting chart indicate the size of the cut square (3" = 3" x 3").					
For 1 block:			5"	6¼"	7½"	8¾"	10"	12½"
Light	A: 4		1⅞"	2⅛"	2⅜"	2⅝"	2⅞"	3⅜"
	B: 5		1½"	1¾"	2"	2¼"	2½"	3"
Dark	C: 4		1⅞"	2⅛"	2⅜"	2⅝"	2⅞"	3⅜"
	D: 12		1½"	1¾"	2"	2¼"	2½"	3"

Try this: Reverse the lights and darks.

☐ Square(s)   ◩▶◺ Square(s) cut once diagonally to make half-square triangles   ⊠▶◸ Square(s) cut twice diagonally to make quarter-square triangles   ▭ Rectangle(s)

Wonder Lake

8-Unit Grid

Color Illustration: page 29

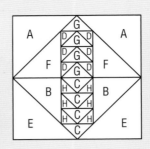

| | | | | FINISHED BLOCK SIZE | | | | | |
| | | | | Single dimensions in the cutting chart indicate the size of the cut square (3" = 3" x 3"). | | | | | |
For 1 block:				6"	8"	9"	10"	12"	14"
Light	A: 1			3⅞"	4⅞"	5⅜"	5⅞"	6⅞"	7⅞"
	B: 1			3⅛"	3⅞"	4¼"	4⅝"	5⅜"	6⅛"
	C: 1			2¾"	3¼"	3½"	3¾"	4¼"	4¾"
	D: 3			1⅝"	1⅞"	2"	2⅛"	2⅜"	2⅝"
Dark	E: 1			3⅞"	4⅞"	5⅜"	5⅞"	6⅞"	7⅞"
	F: 1			3⅛"	3⅞"	4¼"	4⅝"	5⅜"	6⅛"
	G: 1			2¾"	3¼"	3½"	3¾"	4¼"	4¾"
	H: 3			1⅝"	1⅞"	2"	2⅛"	2⅜"	2⅝"

Try this: Use the same light for A and D and a different light for B and C.

☐ Light   ⬚ Light 2   ▨ Medium   ▨ Medium 2   ■ Dark

World's Fair Puzzle

8-Unit Grid

Color Illustration: page 29

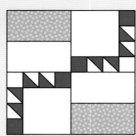
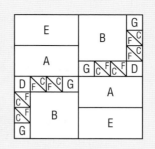
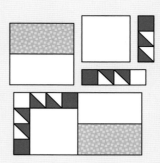

	FINISHED BLOCK SIZE					
	Single dimensions in the cutting chart indicate the size of the cut square (3" = 3" x 3").					
For 1 block:	6"	8"	9"	10"	12"	14"
Light A: 2 ▢	2" x 3½"	2½" x 4½"	2¾" x 5"	3" x 5½"	3½" x 6½"	4" x 7½"
B: 2 ▢	2¾"	3½"	3⅞"	4¼"	5"	5¾"
C: 4 ◹→◺	1⅝"	1⅞"	2"	2⅛"	2⅜"	2⅝"
D: 2 ▢	1¼"	1½"	1⅝"	1¾"	2"	2¼"
Medium E: 2 ▢	2" x 3½"	2½" x 4½"	2¾" x 5"	3" x 5½"	3½" x 6½"	4" x 7½"
Dark F: 4 ◹→◺	1⅝"	1⅞"	2"	2⅛"	2⅜"	2⅝"
G: 4 ▢	1¼"	1½"	1⅝"	1¾"	2"	2¼"

Try this: Use a different medium in every block.

Zigzag

5-Unit Grid

Color Illustration: page 29

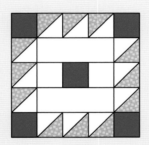
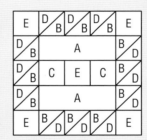
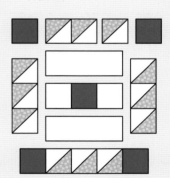

	FINISHED BLOCK SIZE					
	Single dimensions in the cutting chart indicate the size of the cut square (3" = 3" x 3").					
For 1 block:	5"	6¼"	7½"	8¾"	10"	12½"
Light A: 2 ▢	1½" x 3½"	1¾" x 4¼"	2" x 5"	2¼" x 5¾"	2½" x 6½"	3" x 8"
B: 6 ◹→◺	1⅞"	2⅛"	2⅜"	2⅝"	2⅞"	3⅜"
C: 2 ▢	1½"	1¾"	2"	2¼"	2½"	3"
Medium D: 6 ◹→◺	1⅞"	2⅛"	2⅜"	2⅝"	2⅞"	3⅜"
Dark E: 5 ▢	1½"	1¾"	2"	2¼"	2½"	3"

Try this: Reverse the mediums and darks in every other block.

▢ Square(s)	◹→◺ Square(s) cut once diagonally to make half-square triangles	⊠→◹◺ Square(s) cut twice diagonally to make quarter-square triangles	▭ Rectangle(s)

Assembling Your Quilt

Squaring Up Blocks

Some quiltmakers find it necessary to trim or square up their blocks before they assemble them into a quilt top. If you trim, be sure to leave ¼"-wide seam allowances beyond any points or other important block details that fall at the outside edges of the block.

Distorted blocks often can be squared up with a little judicious pressing. Cut a piece of plastic-coated freezer paper to the proper size (finished block size plus seam allowance) and iron the freezer paper to your ironing board cover, coated side down. Align block edges with the edges of the freezer-paper guide and pin. Gently steam press. Allow the block to cool before removing pins.

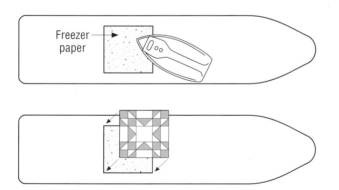

Freezer paper

Straight Sets

In straight sets, blocks are laid out in rows that are parallel to the edges of the quilt. Constructing a straight-set quilt is simple. When you set blocks side by side without sashing, stitch them together in rows. Join the rows to complete the patterned section of the quilt. If you are using alternate blocks, cut or piece them to the same size as the primary blocks (including seam allowance). Lay out the primary and alternate blocks in checkerboard fashion, stitch them into rows, and join the rows.

When setting blocks together with plain sashing, cut the vertical sashing pieces the same length as the blocks (including seam allowance) and the desired finished width, plus seam allowance. Join the sashing pieces and the blocks to form rows, starting and ending each row with a block. Join the rows with long strips of the sashing fabric, cut to the same width as the shorter sashing pieces. Make sure the corners of the blocks are aligned when you stitch the rows together. Add sashing strips to the sides of the quilt top last.

If your sashing includes corner squares of a color or fabric different from the rest of the sashing (sashing squares), cut the vertical sashing pieces and join them to the blocks to form rows, starting and ending each row with a sashing piece. Cut the horizontal sashing pieces the same size as the vertical pieces. Cut sashing squares to the same dimensions as the width of the sashing pieces and join them to the horizontal sashing pieces to make sashing strips, starting and ending each row with a sashing square. Join the rows of blocks with these pieced sashing strips.

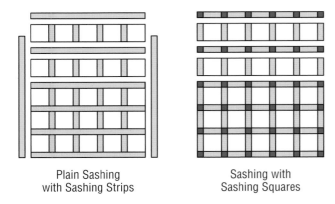

Plain Sashing
with Sashing Strips

Sashing with
Sashing Squares

On-Point Sets

Quilts that are set on point are constructed in diagonal rows, with pieced half blocks and quarter blocks or plain setting triangles added to complete the sides and corners of the quilt. If you haven't already done so, sketch your quilt on a photocopy of one of the quilt-plan work sheets (pages 139–140) so that you can see how the rows go together and how many setting pieces you need.

Plain setting triangles can be quick-cut from squares. You will always need four corner triangles. To maintain straight grain on the outside edges of the quilt, these should be half-square triangles. Two squares cut to the proper dimensions, and then cut once diagonally, will yield the four half-square triangles needed for the corners.

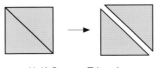

Half-Square Triangles
for Corners

Check your quilt sketch to see how many side triangles you need. To maintain straight grain on the outside edges of the quilt, use quarter-square triangles. A square cut to the proper dimensions and cut twice diagonally will yield four quarter-square triangles. Divide the total number of triangles needed by four, round up to the next whole number, then cut and divide that many squares. In some cases, you will have extra triangles to set aside for another project.

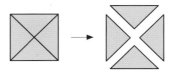

Quarter-Square Triangles
for Sides

How do you determine the proper cutting dimensions for these squares? The calculations are based on the finished size of the blocks, and they vary, depending on whether the blocks are set side by side or are separated by sashing.

For on-point sets where the blocks are set side by side with no sashing, determine the proper dimensions to cut the squares as follows:

Corners: Divide the finished block size by 1.414. Add .875 (for seams). Round the result up to the nearest ⅛" (decimal-to-inch conversions appear on page 12). Cut two squares to that size; cut the squares once diagonally.

Sides: Multiply the finished block size by 1.414. Add 1.25 (for seams). Round the result up to the nearest ⅛". Cut squares to that size; cut the squares twice diagonally. Each square yields four triangles.

For on-point sets where the blocks are separated by sashing, determine the proper dimensions to cut the squares as follows:

Corners: Multiply the finished width of the sashing by 2. Add the finished block size. Divide the result by 1.414, then add .875 (for seams), and round up to the nearest ⅛" (decimal-to-inch conversions appear on page 12). Cut two squares to that size; cut the squares once diagonally.

Sides: Add the finished width of the sash to the finished size of the block. Multiply the result by 1.414, add 1.25 (for seams), and round up to the nearest ⅛". Cut squares to that size; cut the squares twice diagonally. Each square yields four triangles.

On-Point Assembly

As noted in the previous section, quilts laid out with the blocks set on point are constructed in diagonal rows. To avoid confusion, lay out all the blocks and setting pieces in the proper configuration before you start sewing. In an on-point set where blocks are set side by side without sashing, simply pick up and sew one row at a time. Then join the rows. Trim and square up the outside edges after the rows are sewn, if needed.

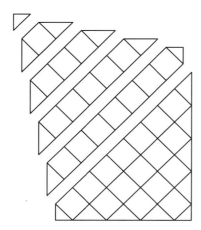

The assembly order for on-point sets that include sashing is a little more complex. You can see from the drawing below that the side setting triangles span a block plus one sashing strip, and the corner triangles span a block plus two sashing pieces. Lay out your blocks, sashing pieces, and setting triangles before sewing so that you can see exactly what pieces constitute each row—or make a photocopy of your work sheet and slice it into diagonal rows. Once you join the pieces into rows, start joining the rows from the bottom-right corner and work toward the center. When you reach the center, set that piece aside and go to the top-left corner, again working toward the center. Add the top-right and bottom-left corner triangles last, after the two main sections have been joined.

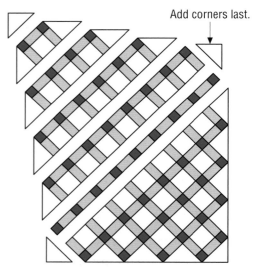

Add corners last.

Assembly Diagram
for On-Point Set with Sashing

Borders

Most quilters frame the patterned sections of their quilts with plain or pieced border strips. Borders with straight-cut corners are suitable for most quilts, but you may wish to add borders with corner squares or with mitered corners.

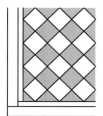  

Straight-Cut Corners   Corner Squares   Mitered Corners

Because extra yardage is required to cut borders on the lengthwise grain, plain border strips commonly are cut along the crosswise grain and joined end to end when extra length is needed. These seams should be pressed open for minimum visibility. Prepare border strips a few inches longer than you think you'll need; trim them to the proper length once you know the actual dimensions of the patterned section of the quilt. Determine the proper length by measuring across the patterned section at the center, not at the outside edges! The outside edges often measure longer than the quilt center due to stretching during construction; if you use these measurements, you are likely to end up with rippled borders and an oddly shaped quilt.

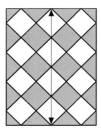 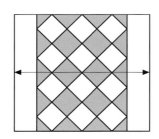

Measure length at center.   Measure width at center after adding side borders.

Borders with Straight-Cut Corners

To make a border with straight-cut corners, measure the length of the patterned section of the quilt at the center, from raw edge to raw edge. Cut two border strips to that measurement and join them to the sides of the quilt with a ¼"-wide seam, matching the ends and centers and easing the edges to fit. Then, measure the width of the quilt at the center from edge to edge, including the border pieces that you just added. Cut two border strips to that measurement and join them to the top and bottom of the quilt, matching ends and centers and easing as necessary.

Borders with Corner Squares

To make a border with corner squares, measure the length and width of the patterned section of the quilt at the center, from raw edge to raw edge. Cut two border strips to the lengthwise measurement and join to the sides of the quilt with a ¼"-wide seam, matching the ends and centers and easing the edges to fit. Then cut two border strips to the original crosswise measurement, join corner squares to the ends of the strips, and stitch these units to the top and bottom of the quilt, matching ends, seams, and centers, and easing as necessary.

Borders with Mitered Corners

To make mitered corners, first estimate the finished outside dimensions of your quilt including borders. Cut border strips to this length plus at least ½" for seam allowances; it's safer to add 2" to 3" to give yourself some leeway. If your quilt is to have multiple borders, sew the individual strips together and treat the resulting unit as a single piece for mitering.

Mark the centers of the quilt edges and the centers of the border strips. Stitch the borders to the quilt with a ¼"-wide seam, matching the centers. The border strip should extend the same distance at each end of the quilt. Start and stop your stitching ¼" from the corners of the quilt. Press the seams toward the borders.

Lay the first corner to be mitered on the ironing board, pinning as necessary to keep the quilt from pulling and the corner from slipping. Fold one of the border units under at a 45° angle. Work with the fold until any seams or stripes meet properly; pin at the fold, then check to see that the outside corner is square and that there is no extra fullness at the edges. When everything is straight and square, press the fold.

Starting at the outside edge of the quilt, center a piece of 1"-wide masking tape over the mitered fold. Remove pins as you apply the tape.

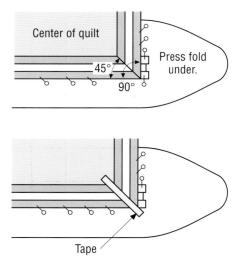

Unpin the quilt from the ironing board and turn it over. Draw a light pencil line on the crease created when you pressed the fold. Fold the center section of the quilt diagonally from the corner, right sides together, and align the long edges of the border strips. Stitch on the pencil line, then remove the tape. Trim the excess fabric and press the seam open. Repeat these steps for the remaining three corners.

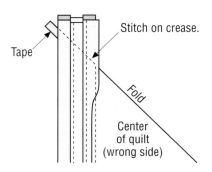

Finishing Your Quilt

As promised, I have taken you from blocks through borders, from the germ of an idea to a completed quilt top. If you need help with marking, layering, quilting, and binding your creation, there are many excellent references that describe the basic techniques. I recommend the "Finishing Your Quilt" section of *Triangle-Free Quilts* (Martingale & Company, 2002).

Work Sheets for Straight Sets

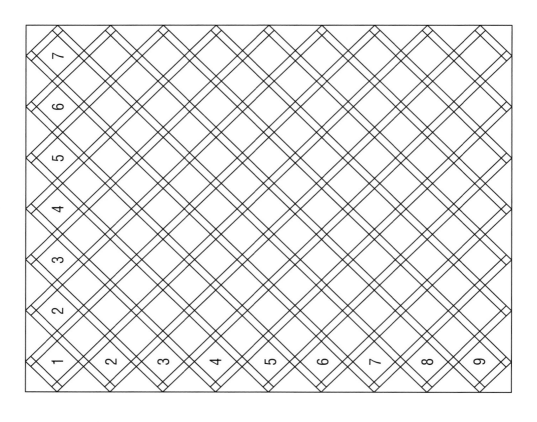

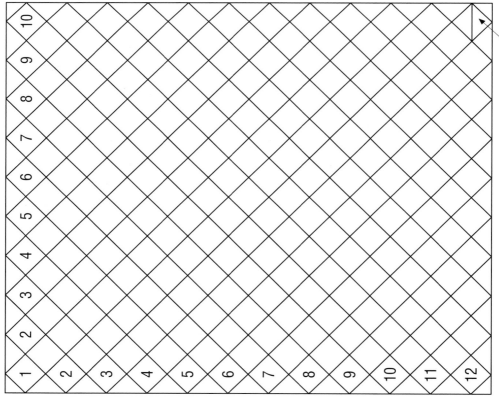

To find finished diagonal measurement of block, multiply finished block size by 1.414.

Block Index

Bibliography

Beyer, Jinny. *The Quilters Album of Blocks and Borders.* McLean, Va.: EPM Publications, 1980.

Bonesteel, Georgia. *Lap Quilting with Georgia Bonesteel.* Birmingham, Ala.: Oxmoor House, 1982.

Brackman, Barbara. *Encyclopedia of Pieced Quilt Patterns.* Paducah, Ky.: American Quilter's Society, 1993; originally published by Prairie Flower Publishing, 1984.

Central Oklahoma Quilters Guild. *Ultimate Illustrated Index to the Kansas City Star Quilt Pattern Collection.* Oklahoma City: 1990.

Goldberg, Rhoda Ochser. *The New Quilting & Patchwork Dictionary.* New York: Crown, 1988.

Gutcheon, Beth. *The Perfect Patchwork Primer.* New York: D. McKay, 1973.

Gutcheon, Beth, and Jeffrey Gutcheon. *The Quilt Design Workbook.* New York: Rawson, 1976.

Havig, Bettina. *Carrie Hall Blocks.* Paducah, Ky.: American Quilter's Society, 1999.

Hopkins, Mary Ellen. *The It's Okay If You Sit On My Quilt Book.* Atlanta, Ga.: Yours Truly, 1982.

Malone, Maggie. *1001 Patchwork Designs,* New York: Sterling, 1982.

McCloskey, Marsha. *100 Pieced Patterns for 8" Quilt Blocks.* Seattle, Wash.: Feathered Star Productions, 1992.

_____. *Marsha McCloskey's Block Party: A Quilter's Extravaganza of 120 Rotary-Cut Block Patterns.* Emmaus, Pa.: Rodale Press, 1998.

McKim, Ruby Short. *101 Patchwork Patterns.* New York: Dover, 1962.

Mills, Susan Winter. *849 Traditional Patchwork Patterns: A Pictorial Handbook.* Mineola, N.Y.: Dover, 1989.

Rehmel, Judy. *The Quilt I.D. Book.* New York: Prentice Hall, 1986.

Stone, Clara. *Practical Needlework: Quilt Patterns.* Boston: C.W. Calkins, 1906.

Yoshitake, Yasuko. *Quilt Blocks 1.* Kyoto, Japan: Kyoto Shoin, 1994.

_____. *Quilt Blocks 2.* Kyoto, Japan: Kyoto Shoin, 1994.

_____. *Quilt Blocks 3.* Kyoto, Japan: Kyoto Shoin, 1994.

About the Author

Judy Hopkins is a prolific quiltmaker whose fondness for traditional design goes hand in hand with an unwavering commitment to fast, contemporary cutting and piecing techniques. Judy has been making quilts since 1980 and working full-time at the craft since 1985. Her primary interest is in multiple-fabric quilts; most of her pieces are inspired by classic quilts in a variety of styles. Her work has been seen in numerous exhibits and publications.

Writing and teaching are by-products of Judy's intense involvement in the process of creating quilts. She is author of *Triangle-Free Quilts, Around the Block Again, Around the Block with Judy Hopkins*, and coauthor (with Nancy J. Martin) of *101 Fabulous Rotary Cut Quilts*. Judy especially enjoys working with scraps. Faced with a daunting accumulation of scraps and limited time with which to deal with them, she started looking for ways to apply quick cutting methods to scrap fabrics. This led to the design of Judy's popular ScrapMaster ruler, a tool for quick-cutting half-square triangles from irregularly shaped scraps, and the accompanying *Blocks and Quilts* for the ScrapMaster series.

Judy lives in Juneau, Alaska, with her husband, Bill. She has two grown daughters and five adorable and brilliant grandchildren, who keep her busy making quilts.